A SCHOLAR'S TALE

A Scholar's Tale

INTELLECTUAL JOURNEY OF A
DISPLACED CHILD OF EUROPE

GEOFFREY HARTMAN

FORDHAM UNIVERSITY PRESS ┃ NEW YORK 2007

Library of Congress Cataloging-in-
Publication Data

Hartman, Geoffrey H.
A scholar's tale : intellectual
journey of a displaced child of
Europe / Geoffrey Hartman.—1st
ed.
    p. cm.
Includes bibliographical
references.
ISBN-13: 978-0-8232-2832-4
(cloth : alk. paper)
  1. Hartman, Geoffrey H.
  2. Critics—United
States—Biography. 1. Title.
PN75.H33A3   2007
801'.95092—dc22
[B]

                   2007029313

Printed in the United States of
America
09 08 07   5 4 3 2 1
First edition

For Renée

CONTENTS

vii

Having written essays for more than fifty years, and seen the coming and going of critical movements during that time, I thought it might interest both suspicious and benevolent readers to view the personal impact these movements have had on someone who cannot call himself a theorist but who has been an engaged observer devoted to literary and cultural matters. These autobiographical reflections, begun in 2004, finished in 2006, say something about the growth of a critic's mind. They occasionally lean on previous fragments, such as my "Polemical Memoir" prefacing *A Critic's Journey* of 1999; "A Life of Learning," the American Council of Learned Societies annual Haskins Lecture in 2000; and the title essay of *The Longest Shadow: In the Aftermath of the Holocaust* (1996). What I offer here is not a "Life" in the conventional sense but a memoir focusing on my intellectual development.

The *Biographia Literaria* of Coleridge has often been in my mind. There is a certain clutter and clotting in him too, but his opinions are firmer, and they focus principally on Wordsworth and Shakespeare, with recourse, when necessary, to the standards of Aristotle, and the impact, which he analyzes—and resists—of Locke, and such contemporary philosophers as Hartley and Fichte. But he avoids what is central to my own effort: commenting on one's own books. I suspected too late that I might be trying to forestall interpretation or judgment. That is not what I had in mind.

"Why have I seen what I have seen," Ovid's Actaeon cries. Many feel that way, experiencing daily not only what happens in their immediate neighborhood but also, via the media, astonishing or wounding things from elsewhere. My endeavor is neither to astonish nor to revive difficult memories. It is motivated, rather, by a defense of literary studies in their increased scope and variety. In short, let the reader beware: this is not a spectacular story but an academic one. Being a horse of instruction rather than a tiger of wrath, I embody very little of what Blake advises in his "Proverbs of Hell." But I do take comfort in one axiom of his: "No bird soars too high, if he flies with his own wings."

I acknowledge with pleasure the encouragement of Helen Tartar, editorial director of Fordham University Press, and perceptive readers of the book in manuscript form, Peter Cole, Marianne Hirsch, and Marilyn Gaull. My wife, Renée, to whom the book is dedicated, helped to make it a labor of love.

GEOFFREY HARTMAN
January 2007

A SCHOLAR'S TALE

"Write something European."
    —Greta Garbo, in Hollywood, to Salka Viertel

"Going where? Just going. That would be enough."
    —Robert Penn Warren, "Covered Bridge"

". . . as for their fingers, they were enveloped in some myth."
    —Herman Melville, *The Confidence Man*

"We're here to hunt. Not to write our memoirs."
    —The General, in Jean Renoir, *Rules of the Game*

Trajectory, itinerary, journey.[1] These are attractive and deceptive metaphors. They suggest a chosen or predetermined path, with a distinctive goal and course corrections. This is bound to lead to ego fiction. Was the classifier at Barnes and Noble right, the one who marketed *A Critic's Journey*, my book of selected essays, under "Travel"?

Yet I doubt that the writings of a displaced European who was nine years old when he left Germany can be likened to a travelogue, fictionalized or not, except that cultural differences continue to intrigue him. ("European" is a bit of exaggeration to describe a German waif, but that persona-image somehow took over after I had come of age in America.) More appropriate in the long run is to apply to the shape of his various essays John Crowe Ransom's ironic description of poetry: logical structure wedded to irrelevant texture.

I will reflect, then, on both the continuities and shifts or discontinuities in my career. Always keeping in mind, however, Adam's admission in Milton's *Paradise Lost*: "Who himself beginning knew?" The very genre of autobiography tempts us to invent a clear, even traumatic (therefore fallible) point of origin, instead of considering that we may have drifted into our identity, or that we continue to construct it. The fingers that write (and pick the pockets of previous writers) are always enveloped in some myth. Wordsworth, in *The Prelude*, expands Adam's caution:

Who knows the individual hour in which
His habits were first sown, even as a seed,
Who that shall point, as with a wand, and say
"This portion of the river of my mind
Came from yon fountain?"
(*The Prelude* [1805] 2.211–15)

**Displacements
and continuities.**

Without trying to get back to a genesis moment that might have started a fateful chain reaction, I discern some uncanny continuities. For many years I hoarded an essay called "Cultural Memory and the Passion Narrative." The Passion narrative has received a new injection of relevance through the wide appeal (at least in America) of Mel Gibson's film *The Passion of the Christ*. Only when I began thinking back did it come to me that in the late 1950s, aiming to be a poet, I actually wrote fragments of a Passion Play removed from its Christian context and adapting the words of a Holocaust survivor. Because of my instinctive antitheatrical prejudice, the play was meant to be recited rather than acted. Its form approximated a Greek tragedy, featuring a chorus, a protagonist bent on self-sacrifice, and a survivor's flashback conversation with a Nazi officer in a death camp.

That this play, and another on the biblical figure of Saul, failed to be completed, was not caused by the pains of what Eva Hoffman's *Lost in Translation* calls "Life in a New Language." Yet the very attempt to write ambitiously *was* affected by my displacement. Exposed at an early age to the great literary exemplars of Britain, my first country of adoption, I developed a love of literature, influenced more by its architectonic and musical qualities than by a mature content I could barely understand. I did not lose anything in being translated from one culture to another, but gained a new language without rejecting my mother tongue, which I no longer spoke but preserved in silence together with the image of my absent mother.

I also gained (if it was a gain) a hankering after literary sublimities I could not live up to, even in maturity. Without neglecting what Blake called "the rough basement" of vernacular speech, I was drawn in terms of formal conceptions to the high Romantic mode as well as to the mystery of biblical figures that had to shoulder the burden of a divine election.

A second continuity needs a somewhat lengthy prologue. I tend to prefer instances of eccentric interpretation to the task of chastening these by criteria of correctness. It is not so much a libertarian attitude that motivates me as the pleasure of allowing texts to lead my thoughts, and to work them through collectively in class. When deciding among interpretive choices, I abandon the rejected or marginal ones only reluctantly. Interpretation, I feel, should be a feast, not a fast.

This interest in the process of interpretation, more than in proving or fighting for a particular view, led to a "Mikado"-like "object all sublime" for my studies. Actually, a second one. The first I've already mentioned in passing. Had you asked me in my twenties the equivalent of "What do you want to be when you grow up," I would have answered, "a teacher of literature." The more honest reply was, however, "a poet." Still, returning to the university after two painful and tedious, if also at times hilarious, years as a draftee in Uncle Sam's army (1953–55), I decided to write a History of Interpretation—not just to cover its present, mainly secular phase, but also to respect the eight-ninths of a hidden iceberg, primarily a religious mass often overlooked by modern literary thinkers.

I had become fascinated by Christian as well as Rabbinic exegeses: their extravagance, daring, and perverse elaboration (or so it seemed) of sacred texts. I soon realized my lack of resources for such a history, and, in order to make some headway on the Rabbinic side, spent the mosquito-filled summer of 1957 at the Jewish Theological Seminary in New York.[2] It only confirmed that I would never make enough headway, given my advanced age at the time—all of twenty-seven.

To get into Talmud and the accompanying corpus of midrashic texts, you must begin training as early as a ballerina: at age seven, say, not twenty-seven. Yet Akiba, who became the patron sage of *Akiba's Children*, my only book of verse,[3] was probably close to middle age when, as it is told, this illustrious rabbi, once an illiterate peasant, eavesdropped on a school to begin his education.

Given my own belatedness, and that I'd have to be more proficient at ancient and modern languages, I relinquished the projected History of Interpretation. Yet for many years—at least until *Midrash and Literature* (1986) was published—I continued a scholarly flirtation with the freer form of Midrash, *midrash aggada*.[4] Its imaginative development even within the framework of legal issues prepared me for a broader engagement with Judaic studies, which I helped to organize at Yale in the early 1980s.

The uncanny continuity for which the above is prefatory involves ancestry. While a visiting professor at the

University of Zürich, I recalled that my maternal grandfather—a teacher of religion at the oldest German Jewish school, the Frankfurt Philantropin, established in 1804, and who died when I was a year old—had studied for a time at Zürich before receiving his doctorate. I consulted Zürich's municipal library, and, behold, it had his dissertation, *The Book of Ruth in Midrash-Literature*.[5] Returning to Yale, I hastened to look in *its* library, and . . . found the same booklet right there.

Were there sharp turns in my self-image or career consciousness? I was blessed with a surprising lack of career thinking during my first appointment at Yale (1955–62), perhaps because of an alternate and very strong, if inchoate, sense of vocation. That sense arrived early yet never tangled enough with academic politics or polemics to accrue missionary intensity.

The sense of vocation. From England to America. Queens College, Yale, the army.

Where my wish to teach and study literature came from, I do not know to this day, but once on that path nothing could divert me. However obscure the motivating source, several factors contributed to self-reliance. With over twenty boys, I had been evacuated from Frankfurt in March 1939, on a "Kindertransport." We were resettled in a small English village, a dependency of the Waddesdon Manor and its owners, James and Dorothy de Rothschild, who supported the refugees. My mother had left for America in December 1938, shortly after the pogrom of *Kristallnacht*, intending I should join her as soon as a visa could be obtained. My grandmother, already ill, did not escape and died in Theresienstadt. My father, long divorced, managed to emigrate to Argentina.

5

Because of the war and the submarine menace, I was unable to join my mother until August 1945. I was then close to sixteen and eager to continue my education. But she worked all day for subsistence wages and basically I had to look after myself.

When I arrived in New York (I still remember hearing on the ship about the first atom bomb), demobilization had begun and the City Colleges had room only for the returning soldiers. I worked part time at Gimbel's and took evening courses at Hunter College: the only male, except the teacher, in my classes. (At least that's how I remember it.) That my full-time formal education was interrupted only spurred me on. Eventually admitted to Queens College, CUNY, I would get up at dawn for an extra hour of language study, as if, in the morning freshness, Spanish, Greek, and Italian depended on me alone. They now lurk dusty, reproachful, and generally unused in a corner of my mind. A superb teacher, Konrad Gries (we should name our teachers, all the more when they do not achieve fame through publication), made every stage of Greek an acquisition of delight, and before the year was out his handful of students began to read Homer.

This instinctive love of learning must have already been fostered by my attempt to escape the unhappy atmosphere of the "orphanage" in England. It was not an unkind place, but neither was there much affection. I managed to be away as much as possible, not only by wandering in the countryside or the magical spaces of the Rothschild park with its deer and horses and sturdy old trees good for climbing, but also by traveling every morning to Aylesbury Grammar School with Raymond Tissot, the son of the Rothschilds' chef and my only close friend.

The school, which accepted me on the basis of an exam administered at the age of ten or eleven, had quite a few caring—though strict—teachers, especially in French and English. I threw myself into schoolwork but also, despite not being tall or hefty, into the bruising game of rugby.

In dreams of Aylesbury I find myself back on its main street, hungrily scouting the stores for off-the-ration candy splinters (the candy ration in those war years was two ounces a week) retrieved from the bottom of large glass containers. Or purchasing a newspaper funnel of greasy crumbs, leftovers from fish and chips, or even, with a sixpence diverted from lunch money, acquiring stamps at Weatherby's for my skimpy collection. Weatherby's was the local bookshop where I also picked up my earliest Penguin and Pelican paperbacks.

At "The Cedars," as our communal home was called, taking its name from the two stately trees at its entrance, my toys were stamps, a few books, marbles, and a chess set, all kept in an open cubby hole. The Cedar Boys had no indoor amusements except cards, marbles, and tiddly-winks. We also played table tennis avidly or used that same table for mock soccer games with a shirt button as a ball and filed-down suit buttons activated by the tiddly-winks as players. Then there was "conkers," in which chestnuts on a string were arrayed in ferocious battles, each warrior nut trying to crack the other until the victorious veteran itself cracked and had to be discarded.

My hang for independence could cause academic trouble. To move forward again to Queens College: at that time the school had a qualifying examination prior to graduation in one's major (mine was comparative literature). It consisted of three essay questions to be answered in a certain number of hours. I got so involved in the first question that I spent most of my time on it, barely finished the second, and had to leave out the third. One of the teachers (with a Germanic disposition) wanted to fail me but luckily was dissuaded by the others.

I still remember the reason behind my near downfall. For my first essay I had chosen to write about the Bible passage in which God admonishes Sarah for laughing, after overhearing Him telling Abraham that she would bear a child in their old age. Could one understand so strange a phenomenon as a God at once infinitely far away and yet so near he hears Sarah laugh and reproaches her? Or that so much should be inflicted on Job, on the Single One (to adopt Martin Buber's Kierkegaardian concept), even if the event was staged, and redeemed, by the sublime pathos of his questions to God? The nonsublime *Wiedergutmachung* at the end, restoring thousands of sheep, cattle, she-asses, and children, did not help my perplexity.

Puzzled and fascinated, it was not till I read Yehuda Halevy's *Kuzari* that my sense of being too removed from an original revelation was comforted. Halevy claimed that an uninterrupted tradition was equivalent to direct experience. This eased my own Job-like wish to be affirmed, to stand in the presence—a wish that has never left me. I have kept a belief in the possibility of a direct line to the truth, if only through the medium of literature.

Also contributing to independence was Yale's comparative literature department. I entered it as a graduate student in the fall of 1949. It offered not a doctrinaire program but a "formation" transmitted by markedly cosmopolitan yet very different scholars. Precisely because they—and most of their students—had passed through a terrible war (in my small graduate-school class almost all were veterans or refugees), it seemed necessary to affirm the wealth and worth of a literary inheritance that had brought such a wonderful harvest of modernist works, even though these did not prevent political disaster. It never entered my head to blame them in any way. I was glad they were still there, as if they too had escaped mortal danger.

After Yale, a further spur to independence came from two futile if sporadically funny years of army service. I was drafted in September 1953, at the time of the armistice effectively ending the Korean War, and served until August 1955. But no one seemed to know what to do with a private with a PhD in literature, except to call him Dr. Private. Those years kept me from becoming over-professionalized. The leisure to read whatever I wanted—despite the military's tendency to waste the recruit's time on chickenshit and mock maneuvers—was an exceptional boon. Assigned to West Germany, I became for a few months driver and interpreter for a lieutenant colonel, who was amused to have a Yale graduate at his beck and call, and who himself had almost nothing to do. "Hartman," he jovially said, throwing some charts at me, "reorganize the battalion." I thought of giving literature classes in an Army prison, but one visit made me see the incongruity.

This was also a time when, to counter my military surroundings (I was eventually transferred to Heidelberg, where I had found a job translating and summarizing German newspapers for the army's Public Information Division), I used furloughs to visit many places, including

Sicily, and began writing poetry in all seriousness. Nor was I immune to the charm of Heidelberg, its famous Neckar valley with river, wooded hill, and ruined castle—all of which helped to revive in me, tinged by a melancholy far from vague and sentimental, since the history behind it was real enough, a sense of German Romantic literature, especially its nature-feeling and the recovery of folk and fairy tales. It was an intense period in which I felt that not to be thinking, feeling, writing, was sinful. Was this a version of the perpetual prayer compulsion I later read about?

Early intellectual trends. Distrust of polemics. *The Unmediated Vision*. Religious implication of this first book.

While still in graduate school, I had become an amateur phenomenologist—observing, letting impressions resonate, attentive to the perceptibility of things and the act of becoming conscious of consciousness itself, while not fearing for a core self, that it might be overwhelmed. Although I divined rather than understood Husserl, whatever I did understand was funneled into the dissertation published as *The Unmediated Vision* (1954). It was minimally influenced by my teachers in comparative literature. Yet their high standards and broad perspective left a mark.

The book, concentrating on four modern poets, did not intend to make a polemical contribution to the idea of Modernism. I may have realized, at some level, that the dissertation was reacting to the effort of T. S. Eliot and company to distance themselves from Romantic origins and link up instead with the metaphysical poets of the early seventeenth century. But I was blind to the rationale behind this kind of gaming with one's heritage, and, as I have said, polemics did not attract me then, and still do not.

I am not proud of my temperament. I envy, in fact, combative intellects like Hannah Arendt's, which respond to the pressure of contemporary political events by incisive, even ruthless judgments, with little qualification and no regard for other kinds of intellectual personality. (A famous example is her harsh verdict on Stefan Zweig's autobiography, *The World of Yesterday*, the last book he wrote in his South American exile before he committed suicide in 1942.) I can get angry when sensing personal maliciousness in a destructive evaluation, but not when an explicit and important point is made correcting a writer's nostalgic falsification of the cultural situation (in Zweig's case, his gilded view of the Habsburg empire before 1914) or similar self-deceptions. In caustic judgments there is something cleansing and memorable. I recall how struck I was reading in Karl Mannheim that the aim of polemics was not to win an argument but to annihilate your opponent, that is, put him *hors de combat*. Yet I cannot shake off a sense that while the back and forth of argument is necessary, there are indeterminable situations, and decisiveness should not escalate and become a murderous conviction—as Valéry had the courage to say outright in an essay of 1932, one of several statements on how historical facts could be used (or abused) to justify the most divergent opinions.

What does attract me about polemics I cannot manage: it needs the triple gift of immense culture, argumentative verve, and statecraft, all of which Cicero shows in his *Academica* dialogues. Yet reading certain evaluations, intelligently negative ones like the remarks in Yvor Winters's *Maule's Curse* about Emily Dickinson's "obscurantism," I am also struck by the aptness of what the critic observes in the disparaged poems rather than by the inevitability of the conclusive judgment drawn. I sense a switch that could have been moved to the "on" rather than "off" position to cover the same features. Winters almost grants this, though with an ironic qualification, after calling one of Dickinson's lyrics "abominable." The difficulty, he goes on, is that "even in the poems in which the defects do not intrude . . . one is likely to feel a fine trace of [Dickinson's] countrified eccentricity"; that "margin of ambiguity" is always there, even in her best poems, and yet, he admits, "she is a poetic genius of the highest order, and this ambiguity in one's feelings about her is highly disturbing." This is itself honest criticism of a high order, also of an older order that separated beauties from defects and did not try to reach an understanding of their conjunction. Nothing is interpreted away, everything is clearly judged in an up-or-down way. Nevertheless: the least we can learn from interpretation as an art, as from humanistic discussion in general, is the quirky arbitrariness and relative mortality of judgmental edicts.

Perhaps my predilection for the inclusive rather than exclusive "or" goes to explain being haunted from early on by two stories suggesting the existence of a contrary reality in the form of irreversibles. I must have encountered one of these in a *Märchen* or folktale; the other comes from the *Arabian Nights*. In the former, a stubborn quester demands to find Death in order to question him about how much life he has left. Death appears and takes him to a huge cave where innumerable candles are burning down. Each of these, says Death, is a life. And where am I, says the quester, which one is my life. Here, says Death, and snuffs out his candle.

The second tells of another quester, who must pass many tests to gain his end. One of these confronts him with a room in a palatial building that has a marble floor made of black and white squares, somewhat (I tell myself) like a chessboard. He must pass through the room but knows that stepping on the wrong color is deadly. Everything depends on that first step. In the fleeting image I carry with me, it is unclear whether each further step does not demand an equally fateful choice.

On one issue I was uncompromising: literature was not there to comfort or console. It sustained an aspiration that was surprisingly strict, that felt like an intellectual emotion—an emotion intolerant of banality or sentimentality. I would let nothing stand in the way of a direct, though also meditative, reading. The basic aim behind *The Unmediated Vision*, therefore, was that it would interpret a number of poets from 1800 to 1939 by what I deemed to be an inductive method based solely on their literary writings.

Erich Auerbach, already at Yale in 1950, my second graduate year, helped with the example of *Mimesis*, which used the close reading of a passage as the starting point for insights into a large historical development.[6] Even more important was Auerbach's magnanimous rather than pale cosmopolitanism, his ability to take pleasure in the diversity of the national vernaculars as they developed their own literary canon. When I eventually learned about the Nazi's so-called cleansing of German culture in order to render it purely "Nordic" or "Aryan," it placed the refugee scholars who taught me in an even more appealing light.[7]

In this first book, moreover, there are signs of an attempt to understand the religious imagination. Judaism, to my youthful and adventurous mind, encouraged an unmediated, even risky, relationship to God— unmediated except for a consecrated text. This mindset, I must have thought, resembled that of modern poets. I argued that Wordsworth, Rilke, Valéry, and (from within his strong, sensory *imitatio Christi*) Hopkins were themselves mediators by living the lack of mediation. How else might every idol of the intellect be overcome on the way to what I called "a perfect induction and a faultless faith"? The book's epigraph came from Deuteronomy: "The Lord talked with you face to face in the mount out of the midst of the fire. I stood between the Lord and you at that time, to shew you the word of the Lord: for ye were afraid by reason of the fire, and went not up into the mount" (5:4–5).

Modernist artists, in this view, whether secular or religious, strive to come "face to face." They rely on the plot of the senses and endeavor to look at reality, human or divine, as directly as possible. Yet one of the book's concluding chapters claims that poetry's symbolic process undoes the specificity of the experience undergone in order to gain a "pure representation" or "imageless vision." (What would be left at the end of this *via negativa*, I later wondered.) Mysticism and a desire for purity joined to give that chapter a more than adolescent intensity. I had embarked on a para-Maimonidean quest for an imagination purged of anthropomorphic ideas—and the emotion behind it may also have been indebted to Meister Eckhart. People should not keep out the view, Virginia Woolf once said. That view, "washed in the remotest cleanliness of a heaven / That has expelled us and our images" (Wallace Stevens), offered a solitary reader glimpses of transcendence.

In the Hebrew Bible, moreover, there is the trace of a companion who dwells with God from the Beginning. She is called Wisdom in Proverbs, and this Sophie or Sapientia is especially important for the Jewish Kabbalah. Did that figure, or similar avatars, slip enticingly into my thoughts? Sheer visuality, the light of the senses, while a good thing, was not an end in itself even in the days of my youth; indeed, I associated such organic pleasure with the delight of intellectual discovery. This desire for a union of the sensuous and intellectual was expressed by an emphasis, especially in the Valéry chapter, on poetic images of a glorious body to accompany the intellect of God's partner, the immortal Sophie.

In the ordinary course of things, my wild book would never have made it through the mill of publication reports and committees. But Henri Peyre (more about him later) carried the manuscript personally to the director of Yale University Press, and, after affidavits from my teachers in comparative literature, it was accepted—going out of print in about ten years, having sold a grand total of nine hundred copies.

By the time of *Wordsworth's Poetry* (1964), some naïveté had worn off. I became fully aware of the Anglo-American polemic downgrading Romanticism as naïve, adolescent, self-deluding, un-Modernist. No tough intellectual grace there, no theological challenges, but a too liberal or sentimental or spilt religiosity. In English departments, moreover, including that of Yale, there was little interest in Continental Romanticism's contribution to critical theory. It was my affection, encouraged by René Wellek, for the delayed but extraordinary German renaissance in literature and philosophy at the turn of the eighteenth century (Wellek's first major work was *Kant in England*) that alerted me to the importance of Romanticism and sparked my resistance to any version of intellectual history omitting its contribution.

Coleridge might have fostered a Continental type of philosophic criticism; indeed, parts of Coleridge were abbreviated and adapted to New Critical purposes—without, often, an awareness of how much he had borrowed from German sources.[8] But Coleridge broke off chapter 13 of his *Biographia Literaria*, after clearing his throat (intellectually speaking) in order to define the imagination. He claimed to have received a letter from a friend (a further letter from Porlock, as it were)[9] asking him to cease and desist from cerebral speculations of the Teutonic kind and return to his senses—to what in our time came to be known as *practical* criticism. This move proved to be paradigmatic: it anticipated the aborting in England, and later on in America, of the Continent's fruitful mélange of philosophy and literary criticism—despite the boisterous intervention of Carlyle's *Sartor Resartus*.

Recently, in Terry Eagleton's memoir *The Gatekeeper*, I recognized what kept riling me into the 1970s about

Anglophile attitudes in the field of literary commentary. Eagleton describes his Cambridge supervisor, certainly an intelligent don but antagonistic to the idea of ideas. He did not see the need for them; indeed, writes Eagleton, "I soon discovered that his role as a teacher was to relieve me of my ideas, as the role of a burglar is to rifle your bedroom. . . . If you had presented him with a text containing the secret of the universe, he would have only noticed a displaced semi-colon."

The Englishness of the English was no myth, as I gradually discovered. I already felt it in the reception of *Wordsworth's Poetry*. Unlike in the States, the English reception was downright hostile, as if I had desecrated an idol of the tribe. My argument on Wordsworth's relation to Nature was misunderstood as a thesis-ridden and overintellectualizing deconstruction (although that word was not current at the time) of the poet's love for the English countryside. A barely polite review in the *Times Literary Supplement* did condescend to praise the usefulness of . . . my endnotes. Since word reached me that the anonymous reviewer was Jonathan Wordsworth, on my next trip to England I telephoned him: a stunned silence prevailed, as if the devil himself had called. Then English courtesy came back and I was asked over to his Oxford College office. After a drink or two, and when the ice was broken, he invited me to his home, where the hospitality of Ann Wordsworth (clearly on my side!) and a series of challenging table-tennis games sealed a wary friendship.

I still felt a cultural divide even in 1983, at the Clark Lectures sponsored by Cambridge University's Trinity College, two years after the English faculty's rejection of Colin MacCabe had become a *cause célèbre* debated by the University Senate. I believe I was one of the first American scholars invited to give the lectures, but except for a few young Turks the audience was super polite and not ready to talk about "The Poetical Character," via a close reading of Smart, Collins, and the Romantics, a reading that focused on the vision these poets had of literary history and their own vocation. The American guest was accommodated, however, in a grand bedroom formerly used by the hanging judge on his circuit as well as by Prince Albert, and I did receive charming billets from quite a few in the audience, so perhaps that was the etiquette.

It is hard to see myself as a literary-critical "terrorist," despite having been described as such. What was lively at that time in English studies was motivated by a sociopolitical interest and had mainly leap-frogged over the renaissance of Romanticism at Yale, as well as Derrida's American incursion. During that same Cambridge stay, Terry Eagleton asked me to give a talk at Oxford, and when I arrived at the meeting hall, together with the distinguished Joyce scholar Richard Ellmann, we were confronted by a huge red banner announcing the sponsoring organization and a Cerberus of a cashier at the entrance. I explained who I was and was waved through; as for Ellmann, he indignantly pushed his way in. A surprisingly large audience attended—more the result of organizational skill, I suspect, than my topic or person.

Encroachments by adherents of Kierkegaard, Croce, and Ortega did not fundamentally alter the situation. Edmund Wilson, like T. S. Eliot, had no patience with a German-type philosophy's dominant influence on the Continent. Despite his lively account of Lenin in *To the*

Finland Station, Wilson confessed: "I have never done anything with German philosophy, and can't bear it." A philosophical admixture would not return until well after the Second World War, when Sartre's Marxist and existentialist thought proved somewhat exportable, more than Heidegger, who attracted only a small coterie. Georg Lukacz became well known, Walter Benjamin and Theodor Adorno were gradually translated, and—*enfin*—Derrida appeared. But these incursions merely sparked a war against theory.

It is not totally clear to me why I felt aggrieved by the open animosity to the post- (rather than neo-) Kantian philosophy displayed by so many in literary studies. True, that animosity was rightly blamed for helping to impoverish Anglo-American criticism, but it could have been shrugged off as a defense against the accusation of intellectual fraud or obscurantism. Zealous to guard the small autonomy of their academic province, literary devotees were constantly fighting charges of lacking a real function. What were we basically? Teachers providing a safe environment for hormonal youngsters whose atrocious habits of speech and writing had to be straightened out. All the rest was . . . rhetoric. Public opinion still regards literary dons with bemused suspicion, as akin to prayerful priests who once upon a time assured a country's providential quota of rain and fertility.

An interest in aesthetics provided an exception to the animosity toward philosophical thought. Kant's Third Critique on the Aesthetic Judgment kept its interest. The neo-Kantianism of Ernst Cassirer had an impact on Susanne Langer and stimulated formalist attempts to define the literary object's literariness as well as expanding interest in its anthropological dimension. The "empiricists" among us, moreover, respected ordinary-language philosophy, however lean its aesthetic yield. It seemed less problematic and more scientific than the speculative, intricate, and dialectical kind of thinking that used a Hegelian hermeneutic to understand literature from a mediated, especially socioeconomic perspective. Although such a perspective soon returned in force, nourished largely by neo-Marxism and the spreading influence of Adorno and Benjamin, Anglo-American literary studies, rejecting most foreign ideas as fustian, would claim to be "practical," in touch with sensible words and less grounded in theory—Aristotle's *Poetics* always excepted. Indeed, there was a return, also nourished by Coleridge's *Biographia Literaria*, to Aristotle, whose analytic precepts revived under the auspices of Ronald Crane and the "Chicago School."

While for me the large ideas of German philosophy were innocent until proven guilty, for many others they were guilty until proven innocent. Nietzsche was a nihilist, Hegel the father of totalitarianism. Such were the simplifications that any scrupulous reading could explode easily enough.

It depended, of course, on what motivated one's reading. Filled with curiosity rather than dread, I underestimated the driven temperament of crisis-thinkers who sought a decisive guide or inspiring influence. My previously mentioned pleasure in the process of interpretation and the discipline of close reading still sought to overcome the possible recurrence of all ideological distortions, not only egregious instances like Nazism's defamatory culture war. I was too innocent, in the sense that for a long time I could only puzzle over the fact that modern regimes had adopted—hijacked is a better word—comprehensive philosophies like Nietzsche's, turning them into rigid worldviews to serve the same end as an established religion, a political theology. During the period of the cold war, the "paranoid style" of politics could also affect literary studies—its bad effect was not limited to the Soviet sphere of influence.

There was certainly a move away from innocence in the ten years between *The Unmediated Vision* and *Wordsworth's Poetry*. Their one common element was a simple biographical fact: Wordsworth figured largely in both. My displacement from Frankfurt to Waddesdon and the English countryside of Buckinghamshire made a lonely child appreciate the rural world's companionate presence. Bucks was my Lake District, though with ponds rather than lakes, and not one significant hill, let alone mountain. In that green exile I was obliged to rely on my own thoughts and every English author that grammar school pupils were given to digest. To

Difference of *Wordsworth's Poetry* from my first book. Mediation and "loss of innocence." Attraction to French poetry more than to the novel. Admiration for and difficulty with circumstantial detail.

this day I remember the delight in encountering the essays of Charles Lamb, not only his warm, quirky humor, but a prose style I hoped would help fashion my own.

What also got to me, what fell into me, as it were, was blank verse: that of Shakespeare and Milton as well as Wordsworth. I passed through a stage where everything turned into that measure; it became as natural as breathing, as easy as rap to its performers, although no audience appeared except . . . rabbits in the open fields and a medley of cows.

So there was this tug of a residual, physical memory. But—from where the intellectual change between the two books? I had always paid close attention to style and appreciated European masters of stylistics. In the very poet who naturalized the diction of English poetry, who released it from artificial condensations into a viva voce harmony of thinking and speaking (even if he retained certain devices of declamation), I now began to see what subtlety of thought, sensory dialectics, verbal choices, intertextual echoes, and complex social concerns were embedded in my strong impression of Wordsworth's originality. The Hegelian formula of how history advanced by a synthesis of conflicting ideologies, by distilling a new immediacy from them, made sense—in the realm of nonprogressive poetry, however, rather than Hegel's triumphalist world spirit. The "unmediated" turned out to be a construct, or the historical outcome of an extraordinary individual achievement that included a fortunate forgetfulness or ignorance of historical precursors.

Before I leave this stage of my development, I should note an interest that had less continuity. What mysterious associations made me enjoy French literature as well, especially its nineteenth-century poetry? Perhaps precisely that I had no associations with the language, or that I needed the sense of linguistic flexibility it allowed. There was a phase in early adolescence when I immersed myself in dictionaries, and even our school's Latin Grammar Book. I took to the sound and rhythms of Lamartine, Vigny, Hugo, and Musset. I read them even in preference to the modern French novel.

I also entered the world of the symbolist poets, from Baudelaire to Rimbaud and Valéry, admiring a Modernism that maintained pastoral and classical features despite raw and realistic intuitions. That same residual classicism is glimpsed in what might be called, borrowing from an etiquette in the Jardin du Luxembourg, the "patrimoine végétale" of an art like that of Matisse. Bringing flowers and bodies together, it creates interiorized arabesques more colorful than the sunlight reveals.

Henri Peyre, head of Yale's French Department, feigned shock when I argued in his seminar that Nerval's lyric *Chimères*—"Illusions," as well as mythical creatures part woman part animal, and poems close at times to what was later called "pure poetry"—were worth Proust's *À la recherche du temps perdu*. But my taste remained eclectic: Maurice Scève and Ronsard were as important as Leconte de Lisle, André Gide's sly narratives (who reads them now?) as Balzac's realism, the latter's skill in gradually disclosing, through physiognomic and topographical features, an entire social and psychological world.

Even today I remain awestruck at writers who fill their pages with detailed descriptions—the sounds, for instance, emanating from the African bush, recalled by Doris Lessing in her autobiography. Why do my own pages shy away from such revivals and always try to extract essences? I have too little nostalgia in me, too little anxiety about a certain kind of life passing away.

Lessing regrets that as a young girl she did not record more of her African environment. "We might now have a record of the sounds made by an Africa that no longer exists." Yet like her I do feel a deep regret when the sense of an ending takes hold, jeopardizing through murderous violence and genocide an entire culture, and I fear that so much of value that had been built up cannot be recovered or transmitted. The novel, the memoir, the oral testimony must then supplement history writing, help it to become the bearer of a retrospective "thick description," saving bits and pieces that could seed a renewal.

An example I admire but cannot emulate is Peter Balakian's autobiography, *Black Dog of Fate*. The author, born into an Armenian American family, begins his account by describing his grandmother as she cooks traditional foods, tells folktales to the youngster, and deploys delicious spices. The spicy catalogue he evokes rivals the most poetic of *florilegia*, and he recalls how she recites passages from the Song of Solomon that dwell lovingly on the wordsong of exotic Eastern scents. Starting with these memories of his grandmother, he begins as if unconsciously to piece together his family's past (like the child of Holocaust survivors who gathers hints dropped here and there, or, perhaps, how poems form in the mind), until he finds himself on a "journey into history, into the Armenian genocide." He will be halfway through the book and ready to start graduate school before his grandmother's spice closet opens again, its scents now mingling with the smells and nightmare images of the occulted massacres.

Balakian's recreative gift is to draw a vivid portrait of the America in which he lived, even "the strange sweetness" of his upper-class suburban milieu, and he does not turn against that after his discovery of "the bloody news" of his ancient people's terrible fate in Turkey. Never a topic of conversation at home and buried deep in the family's consciousness, the genocide is eventually and almost incidentally revealed through a young man's reading and the questions that follow. Then what lies encrypted in his grandmother's dreams and strange stories opens up, and he is led to discover contemporary as well as later testimonies of the genocide, including family documents.

But as I read about his journey of discovery, and his retelling of cruel episodes that bring back the degradations, spoliations, deportations, pogroms, tortures, burnings, mass slaughters (no one can miss the Holocaust parallel), I realize how difficult for me it still is to look directly at the Medusa. Perhaps, I think reluctantly, something in me parallels the portrait he offers of Aunt Anna, a scholar of comparative literature. (I was twice invited by her in the 1980s to teach a graduate seminar at NYU, and she would have liked me to explore becoming the chair of her department.) Anna Balakian claimed, passionate as always, that her affection for both symbolist and surrealist movements in France was such that American literature seemed hopelessly worldly! Mallarmé, she insisted, had done away with the circumstantial in poetry. She would not countenance descriptive detail that filled every space with some concrete image or socially engaged observation, as if poetry had to follow William Carlos Williams's "No ideas but in things."

When not busy exploring museums (at this late date providing my first sustained experience of the visual arts) and historic churches like those of Vezelay and Autun, a good part of my Fulbright year in France (1951–52) was spent haunting antiquarian book stores in Paris and then Dijon

Interchapter on
graduate
studies: a
Fulbright year in
France, and
genteel poverty
while at Yale.

(to which I had been assigned by the Fulbright authorities), ferreting out cheap versions of nineteenth-century classics and contemporary critics like Sartre. It was the heyday of existentialism; later, in my first years of teaching, I worked for *Yale French Studies*, an exotic venue where I published on Malraux and Blanchot. Also during those years, Gaston Bachelard, a philosopher turned literary analyst, kept me close not only to the oneiric elements in literature but also to the collusion between imagination, the senses, and the phenomenal ambience of air, earth, fire, water. The "material reveries" of this former philosopher of science, who discovered as many imaginative relationships to the four elements as a vintner detects nuances of flavor in wines from his *terroir*, satisfied a mystical streak in me nearer to Hölderlin's Classical nature-feeling ("Vater Aether!") than to that of Wordsworth.

I still have difficulty letting go of books acquired at that time, despite their wilted, brown, disintegrating paper. But then I have a difficulty disposing of any book: my library, however untidy, is like an embodied memory, a marvelous, personalized RAM. When I browse and discover a tome I had forgotten about, I take special delight in it, while reflecting sadly on everything I cannot hold in mind.

I should also add something about the conditions in which graduate students without means lived during those years. I had a fellowship that covered tuition but barely the most Spartan mode of living. There was no loan program, significant health care, or any assistance except cheap lodging in the Hall of Graduate Studies, where I spent the first two years together with Thomas Whitaker (now an important voice in the "National Initiative" of Yale's New Haven Teacher's Institute, which aims to strengthen teaching through school-university partnerships) and Fredric Will (voluminous poet and aesthetic philosopher), in a narrow suite of three rooms facing a dark alley between our building and a local high school. In this claustrophobic setting, Fred was endlessly brewing coffee while trying to finish reading Balzac or some other comparative literature assignment; Tom, envied for his efficiency by his roommates, was taking turns on the shared hotplate for his watery tea and preparing report after report to satisfy a forced reading march through long English novels.

Horn and Hardart sandwiches from the Automat of that name or a dish of buttered spaghetti in a cheap local bistro were staples. To get extra cash, I capitalized on having directed a play while an undergraduate at Queens College. This allowed me to claim a specialty and hire myself out each year for a few dollars more as a dramatics counselor for young kids in summer camp. (My storytelling experience at camp later served me well as a parent, when, fortified by alliteration, I assuaged the night fears of my son with a saga about Jittery Jacob and his wise hoo-hooing friend Olga the Owl, who lived in the wooded part of the park across the street, while my daughter loved to hear about the sorrows of Dido the Donkey, who always felt lonely and needed her company. After a while, she would ask at bedtime, "Tell me a Dido!")

There were few women students in graduate school, and my "Sophie" was unfindable. Would I have been able to entertain her, even had she appeared? In my thesis year I mowed gardens, waited tables at alumni gatherings, and tutored the children of Yale professors in Latin. Toward the end of that year not enough was left of my fellowship stipend and these extras for the dissertation to be professionally typed, a matter of little more than a hundred dollars. Having no other recourse, I turned to the most generous, intellectually, of my teachers, Henri Peyre. He lent me the money but meant it as a gift. He was surprised, as he later told me, that while in the army I sent him regularly a small amount till the debt was paid off.

Early academic appointments and wanderings. When I left the army in 1955, faculty positions were scarce, but there wasn't as great a crush of aspirants as at present. On the basis of my first book I received a junior appointment at Yale. For reasons I will explain later, I did not like the atmosphere at Yale. While not unfriendly, it was distancing. I was glad for the company of my peers, in particular Harold Bloom, Tom and Liliane Greene, and Harry Berger in English, as well as Dick and Carol Bernstein and the Rortys in philosophy. But except for a few stylized occasions (petite cucumber or liverwurst sandwiches at the chairman's house, a white-glove call of the chair's wife on my wife, and, so far as I remember, one sociable dinner in which the custom still prevailed of the ladies withdrawing into another room after the meal), there was only accidental contact and polite exchanges with the senior faculty during departmental housekeeping events. I recall as exceptional the warmth of Frederick Hilles and his wife Sue, both close friends of Henri Peyre. As for the students: in my first half a dozen years at Yale I taught only undergraduates, and though there was a sprinkling of truly excellent ones, the majority consisted of gentleman C or bare B caliber, who served their time and no doubt had a more lively demeanor outside of class, to judge by the sporting events, the almost weekly migrations to and from women's colleges in the area, the annual panty raids, and *gaudeamus* rumors.

Not particularly sociable myself, I spent most of the time in Yale's wonderful Sterling Library. I could have become a gargoyle in this cathedral. But I did not mind the thought of leaving Yale, and two occasions soon presented themselves.

Patronage was the order of the day and lack of it could prove fatal to a career. Yet it might also be used to circumvent the rules in a generous spirit. What worked in my favor, when Henri Peyre intervened to sidestep those rules, did not always help when exclusivist tendencies kicked in or favorite sons (at that time, inevitably sons) came up for tenure. In 1961, a professor at the University of Chicago, to which I had been invited for a trial year, made it quite clear he opposed me, at least for the time being. "We don't believe in young geniuses here." I would have liked to stay at this university, where I thoroughly enjoyed my first co-ed teaching and even had a following—precisely because I was young—in the one graduate seminar I was allowed. At that time, Chicago's college and the "Division" (basically the graduate school) were still almost separate entities; the college wanted me to stay, but instead of being offered tenure I was asked by the English faculty of the Division to mature another three years before a decision would be made. I returned to Yale, not without, through the years, a lingering nostalgia for Chicago's liveliness, its active Jewish community, and my wish to continue helping with the *Chicago Review*. During that year, it opened its pages to my poetry and published with magical immediacy two essays, one on Virginia Woolf, the other on Maurice Blanchot.

As in the incident enabling the publication of my first book, there were scholars and administrators who took chances. How surprised and excited I was when D. C. Allen, the editor of *English Literary History*, accepted "Milton's Counterplot" (my first article for a learned journal) by return mail with a cordial handwritten note.[10] He had the requisite authority. Similarly, I suspect, I owed my first tenure job, at the University of Iowa, to the forcefulness of John Gerber, the chair of English, who had heard from a colleague at Chicago of what had happened there.

I returned to Iowa in September 2006 to accept a literary criticism prize administered by its Writers' Workshop, and I told the story of how shortly after my arrival at the university in 1962 I received a phone call inviting me to a poker game. I don't know who spread the rumor that I was a professional-grade player (I hadn't played even in the army), and being inclined to take things figuratively, I thought this was a way of saying hello and welcome. When I came to the smoke-filled room, however, there they were, the poker players, waiting for me like for a famous gunslinger in a Western.

Very early in my career, while still an instructor (that rank was dropped only in the 1960s, so that Yale's tenure ladder required up to ten years, four in the instructor rank and generally two three-year terms as assistant professor), I was offered an associate professorship at Kenyon College. I suspect it was at the urging of John Crowe Ransom, who had read *The Unmediated Vision*. Because I wanted to be in the company of graduate as well as undergraduate students, I turned down Kenyon's tempting offer. It was a chancy decision. For a time, however, I maintained contact by reviewing poetry for the *Kenyon Review*.

These details are fairly trivial; I record them because I've occasionally come across younger academics who think my path was strewn with flowers. Or worse: that, as one critic publicly declared, Harold Bloom and I, by devoting ourselves to the Romantics, had "feathered our own nest" instead of (like this 1980s protester) espousing women's studies or similar subjects. In truth, his "radicalism" was more mod and career-propitious at that time than studying the Romantics had been in the 1950s. Despite pioneering work by Northrop Frye and Meyer Abrams, the Romantics were hardly a prestigious field except for editing projects; the academic stock market among Anglophiles was still busy devaluing them in favor of the metaphysical poets, eighteenth-century neoclassicism, and the attempt of T. S. Eliot and fellow Modernists to claim that heritage. It took another decade or two for some brave British souls, like Mary Jacobus, Lucy Newlyn and David Simpson, to appreciate American ventures in the area of Romanticism. These "romantic" escapades were not necessarily less "classical": I admired Randolph Bourne's appropriation of that charged word when he wrote that with Thoreau, Whitman, and Mark Twain, "the revolutionary is coming out into the classic." My own tendency was to turn Europe (more precisely, the Continent) against Englishness—although I never quite outgrew a British fondness for understatement and implication.

Interpretation's variorum. The increasing knowledge-burden. Mediation between American and Continental critical modes becomes a personal mission. Growing separation of scholar/critic and general reader. Pursuing forms in *Beyond Formalism*.

I had marveled, in the introduction to *The Unmediated Vision*, at literary criticism's rich, ungovernable variorum of interpretations. I wanted nothing better than a chance to teach that richness, as if it might restrain dogmatism, or because a sharing of this kind would satisfy my need for community. Some ten years later, I began to be concerned, not just delighted or challenged, by the burden of knowledge weighing on both scholar and creative writer after more than a century of historicism, augmented by the beginnings of a media-accelerated information explosion. To apply a phrase from Shakespeare, such knowledge seemed "corrupted in its own fertility." How could literature, supposedly original and creative, absorb the growing chaos of interpretations and endless arrays of fact? Could poetry remain, as Wordsworth phrased it, "the breath and finer spirit of all knowledge"? Eventually, the anxiety roused by this positivistic inflow made me coin the word "surnomie" as the obverse of Durkheim's "anomie."

The same worry held for the critical essay quickly losing its status as Richard Blackmur's "discourse of the amateur." Important cultural critics were moving into the universities. Compared to the practice not only of a Kenneth Burke, Allen Tate, and Edmund Wilson, operating mainly outside the university, but also of those within it, like Richard Blackmur, Leslie Fiedler, and Lionel Trilling, as well as borderers like Philip Rahv and Alfred Kazin, literary criticism was becoming academized and professionalized. When the Modern Language Association asked me to write for its publication (*PMLA*) on its centenary, I may have made the problem worse by contributing a learned disquisition on the hundred years of literary study since 1883. "The Culture of Criticism" focused on the tension between scholar and educated general reader.

At the same time, I became more aware of my frustrated scientific side, intrigued by the thought that even an entity as complex as a work of art was the elaboration of a basic insight that might be retrieved by studying its manifold verbal expression until everything fell into place. (One of my favorite essays was Valéry's early exposition of the method, in art as in science, of Leonardo.) This treasure hunt was like sifting the variorum of a literary work's interpretations in hope of some ultimate truth, or enjoying botany for providing access to the ingenious and florally dazzling variety of reproductive mechanisms. The treasure was the design itself, the revelation of an order, a startling elemental principle within the apparent disorder. There really were, then, or so I hoped, nonreductive structural discoveries.

Yet once discovered, these did not interpret so much as provide a firmer focus for interpretation. The formal pattern added to the intrigue as well as giving aesthetic pleasure. The fact that different meanings, usually dependent on prior literary passages (on intertextuality), were found layered in a poetic phrase without making it lose its coherence, the miracle of that condensation, of mediatory processes packed, as it were, into the microchip of words, was surely part of literature's power and could either reinforce a particular interpretation or detonate the overtones of several, sometimes disparate, meanings.

Unpacking that effect, of course, required the discovery and deployment of a metalanguage. This set up a further tension within humanistic studies, since to be widely communicated such terms of art had to remain part of the ordinary, affective language, which was relatively "impure," in the sense of unscientific. For my part, I like mixtures, and no doubt took chances relying on the maxim that Nature liked mixtures. Many technical terms of art do gradually become naturalized, absorbed into the vernacular of cultural discourse.

Literary studies, then, entered a stage in which they seemed to gain in complexity what they lost in accessibility. Even Wordsworth's originality, or any such opening of the doors of perception, could not totally transcend the tension between formal elements and the inertial, intricate historicity of language, or other material and institutional forces. I no longer described with gusto and complicity an unmediated vision. Now the inevitability of mediation, perhaps dynamic and progressive, became a challenge. A stubborn trace, an unresolved textual element, responding to new contexts with new meanings, delayed closure.

Concerned with mediation, I also viewed my task as that of a go-between, making Anglo-American literary thought more aware of Continental practices, a motive that led, eventually, to *Criticism in the Wilderness* (1980). I must have harbored an idea of what was European (not just English), in the same way as Kazin was moved from early on by the idea of America. Yet, though committed to literature, during these years I felt in a very personal way a need to apply my interpretive zeal beyond the world of specifically literary instances, for I entertained thoughts of child psychiatry and also made an attempt to enter Yale Law School.

Having argued it was a sign of the Modern to look at the Gorgon of reality without the mirror of Perseus, I now revalued the equivalent of that mirror: the older rhetorical and figurative devices that persisted, though quietly transformed, in Wordsworth. Originality was no longer a heroic dismantling of defenses so that a direct intuition of reality might be achieved. The feared Medusa was no longer identified as historical reality, unexplained and overwhelming, or the paralyzing effect of confronting experience in its immediacy. The danger, in fact, as Hegel had pointed out, lay in the ideal of immediacy itself, its false and purely abstract promise of a cure, the temptation of a premature Absolute. That temptation resembled a gnostic revolt aspiring to the quasi-apocalyptic, explosive "purification" of nature and society.

Mediation and immediacy revalued. The life in forms. Great speculative books. A grand theory about Wordsworth's development. My sensitivity to spirit of place.

The title of my 1970 book, *Beyond Formalism*, had an implicit question mark after it, and pointed to the impossibility of not passing through traditional forms in order to get beyond them.[11] There was a life in forms, as art historians like Focillon demonstrated; "the perished patterns murmur," Emily Dickinson wrote. What I mainly objected to was an increasingly deadening pedagogy that turned the valuable technique of close reading into a myopic shibboleth.

While trying to find the link between Wordsworth's stylistic and psychological development (a kind of sleuthing that emulated, I now suspect, several literary analyses by Leo Spitzer), I continued reading in Freud as well as classical and biblical sources. I ate up every grand theory that came my way. A short catalogue would include Schiller's *Aesthetic Education*, Hegel's *Phenomenology* (my introduction to Hegel was through Wellek's rare comments on the margins of my term papers, including the strange scribble of a word I managed to decipher as "Hegel"), Nietzsche's at once erudite and intuitive *Birth of Tragedy*, Freud's *Totem and Taboo*, Jung's archetypes, the Cambridge (post Frazer) school's recovery of the outlines of a sacred drama behind the categories of Aristotle's *Poetics*, Jane Harrison's *Themis* and Theodor Gasper's *Thespis*, Norman O. Brown's revisionist Freudian *Life Against Death*, close to Herbert Marcuse, Huizinga's *Homo Ludens*, the anti-anthropomorphic teachings of Maimonides in *Guide for the Perplexed*, Martin Buber's lyrical *I and Thou*, Bruno Snell on the origins of self-consciousness in Greece, George Poulet's attempt to find the individual *cogito* of each artist (an Archimedian point of conscious self-projection determining comprehensively an entire oeuvre), Van Gennep's *Rites of Passage*, Propp's *Morphology*, and a (politically reformed?) Mircea Eliade's attempt to bring the mythologies and ritual practices of East and West together. The strength of the ancient literatures, or anthropological revaluations of "primitive" ways of thinking by Claude

Lévi-Strauss, made it hard to believe that proud modernity constituted a radical advance.

My own grand theory traced in Wordsworth's personal history, in the growth of a poet's mind, a recap of archaic structures of sensibility underlying religion's visionary concepts. In the beginning, the poet-to-be is haunted by specific places, charged spots comparable to Jacob's Beit-El. A ruined gallows, a tree, a tower, or other cosmic navel might open into vision. That "one" place could lead to the "One." So that vision would avoid apocalypse, however, and save the common range of visible things, the idea of place had to expand into a concept of Nature as a nurturing and guardian presence. The ancient *genius loci* concept helped, as long as mythic presences called spirits of place were seen as tutelary and inspiring and did not multiply as "godkins and godesslings" (so Coleridge called them) parceling out the One Life in which all things participated. Wordsworth, however, except in early drafts of his autobiographical *Prelude*, rarely extraverted the figure of the *genius loci* so often trivialized in neoclassical poetry. He "grounded" the myth, or "swallowed the formulas," as Yeats would say of his own poetic method.

A profound sense of the local was always part of Wordsworth's numinous experience. How often we read, even today, about a religious manifestation, such as an image of the Virgin showing up in relatively unknown places or amid the most ordinary surroundings! The poet would have rejected such happenings as "superstitious fancies" while accepting them as "local romance." Traditionally, spots marked by a theophany were given a name or a new name and held to be sacred. Even when the experience itself "spoke" darkly, a place name remained, as in the Hebrew Bible, and begot explanatory stories. Not usually a frolicsome bard, Wordsworth plays with that marker of orally transmitted traditions in "Poems on the Naming of Places." But the naming that counted was his detailed capture of the psychological impact and temporal development of haunting sensations associated with the agency of Nature.

The most striking psychological correlate of the episodes Wordsworth called "spots of time" was that during the process of individuation, in which a sense of self (of existential singularity) emerged as the vulnerable center of consciousness, the youngster's feeling of having been singled out is raised to religious pitch by particular, yet often ordinary, scenes. They act on him with admonitory intent and a mute kind of speech. Nature, however, gradually undoes its own arresting effect and frees imagination from fixations. The mature poet gratefully attributes to Nature's own tutelage an interchange of perceptual energies. Nature liberates by mobilizing the other senses—particularly the ear—against a tyrannical, predominating eye.

Was focusing on Wordsworth's near-ecstatic sensitivity to spirit of place motivated by my own displacement? Was there, in a homeless youngster, the hope that England might be his true place and inspiration? Could he sing in a foreign land? I had been brought up in a big city, in Frankfurt, and so, as I have mentioned, my first and lasting experience of open nature was the English countryside during the very time I encountered Wordsworth's poetry.

Making this point, however tentatively, I feel like an imitation Kierkegaard. His "Prelude" to *Fear and*

Trembling shuttles back and forth between the story of Isaac's sacrifice and a narrative of traumatic individuation, of how the child is weaned from mother and father. The role of fear, even terror, experienced early, is remarkable from a developmental point of view. That fear factor often translates into religious awe, into "fear and trembling"—not in my case, however. I was in awe only of creation itself, of what I felt Wordsworth expressed: that a great force was masking itself, or gently deployed its majesty, spreading life in "widest commonality."

I cannot explain why that gentle masking did not morph into a death's head, despite my increasing awareness of the Holocaust and of the always barely controlled predominance of malignancy and outright evil in the world. How much illusion was there in me at that time, how much is there still? Reading Norman Manea's memoir, I suspect that only my having escaped his incomparably severer situation, the Transnistrian labor camp and then the all-pervasive political masquerade of Romanian communism—the mental as well as physical torment he and his family lived through—keeps me today from being oppressed by the disillusioned hope he mentions so often. "I had thought," Manea writes, "I could . . . imagine myself the inhabitant of a language rather than a country."[12] Though I too was bewitched by "the Promised Land, language," and could write about the intricate relation of words and wounds, I did not have to suffer, with little possibility of escape, the political traps of informers or the hysterical rhetoric of betrayer and betrayed.

As my own biobibliographer, I glimpse a common axis in my first two books. The axis is not primarily a theory correlating psychological development and basic religious conceptions. It is bookishness itself: more elegantly stated, the problem of literary mediation. That I find it impossible to empty "mediation" of a religious overtone is frustrating. But, except for a Marxism that, powerfully but too narrowly, reenvisions mediation in terms of the realia of material production and frames the story of human liberty as entailing an emancipation *from* religion as well as *of* religion, there is no way to circumvent what Kenneth Burke in *The Rhetoric of Religion* calls logology: that all words are also about words as generative objects, akin to a Logos fathered "In the Beginning." The anarchist philosopher Proudhon points to a parallel quandary when he laments that language is full of Jove,[13] and Derrida's major effort was spent outwitting the logocentric character of the human sciences without giving up their elaborate written texture.

I may be deceiving myself by viewing the change between these first books as exceptional in my intellectual life. The question comes up whether one can ever read one's own mind. I could be quietly adjusting, smoothing over rifts and contradictory states. My early critique of structuralism, written shortly after the Wordsworth book, emphasized the pain of discontinuity and the folly of viewing time as homogeneous. A recent philosophic dispute divides writers into narrative and episodic types: I would like to be characterized as an admixture, but this evades the troubled sense, while analyzing myself, that different voices within me are always striving for a polyphonic resolution. My work, I have been told, brings in too many references, too many other voices, so that it is often difficult to arrive at a clear sense of where I stand.

There are moments, moreover, in which, when others quote me, I do not immediately recognize my own thoughts. In fact, I sometimes dip into my writings almost in the manner of those who use biblical or Vergilian *sortes*. I do so not to solve a moral or existential quandary but as a kind of reality-testing. Can I still recognize myself? The results are not always comforting. Even should the passage my eyes land on be surprisingly good, I fear it is too good, in the sense that I might not be able to equal it. Suspended between admiration and anxiety, I wonder: Was that really my hand? Did I know what I was saying? At other moments, of course, I regret the blind spots, the inexplicable disregard of this or that forget-me-not detail. I yearn for a theory to justify my return to the same poems with another and yet another interpretation. In the case of Wordsworth, I have developed a half-dozen variant perspectives on his lyrics about Lucy, and I remain unsure they can be reconciled. Are we not always, in fact, rewriting sacred, canonical, or legal texts by reinterpreting them? In appearance we remain the same person, recognizable as such, even at the very moment of death. But when does a text die; do some texts have an infinite capacity for internal change under the synergic pressure of interpretation, while keeping an outward semblance of self-sameness? The kabbalists thought this infinite capacity was a distinguishing property of Scripture.

One factor certainly contributed to the change that took place between my first two books. At Yale, in 1955, I met Harold Bloom, like myself on first appointment, and our

In the Bloom
sephira.
Contrasting
Blake and
Wordsworth.
Martin Buber a
shared
influence.

conversation (which has lasted) made me attend more closely to the example of William Blake and his deceptive use of traditional apocalyptic imagery. A ghostly dialogue started in my mind between Blake and Wordsworth. Allegorists might even say between Bloom and myself.

Blake's incisive and fierce polemics were often directed against a so-called natural religion that apotheosized what was really a second or fallen nature. He felt that such quasi-Druidic worship circumscribed and distorted human perception everywhere. His chariot of fire went forth against all codified, imagination-limiting forms. Established religion had intervened to preempt the human sense of infinity by systematically creating a new set of authoritative chimaeras to regulate the imagination and legitimate the church. Yet Blake also assailed the Enlightenment's unholy trinity of Locke, Voltaire, and Rousseau, in addition to their common enemy, every established priesthood. In critiques of the Enlightenment, before Adorno and Horkheimer, Blake was.

While Nature is as unavoidable in Blake's poetry as in Wordsworth's, each poet's understanding of the necessity of transcending it differed fundamentally. Nature puts me out, Blake famously declared, and an apocryphal story making the rounds at Yale about Bloom, the city boy, his maiden contact with the countryside as a Cornell undergraduate, mimics a Beerbohm cartoon. An already portly figure recoils aghast, seeing his first real-life cow, bull, or horned thing, while the imaginary caption reads, "What is *that*?!"

Blake charged that natural religion—including a Newtonian science that claimed to ascend from an ordered nature to God—fostered a rationing of imaginative energies. Parodying the scientific term, he denounces "ratio" as a false kind of reason that results in a leveling of difference, in the uniformity of "single vision," and in a repressive conspiracy of church and state to enforce limits on an energy that should be "eternal delight." For Wordsworth, however, Nature was an anti-ideology, resisting mechanical schemes of education and encouraging childhood development every which way.

The memory of his "fair seed-time" saved the adult poet from disruptive, quasi-apocalyptic fantasies of political action incited by the French Revolution. Terror of apocalypse, the very thing mocked or reinterpreted by Blake, inspired Wordsworth's retrieval of early, nature-infused, and often underconscious images and led him to emphasize memory in the modern sense of a core of binding and identity-shaping influences. A rediscovery of Nature's persisting influence became for him what Virgil was to Dante's anagogic quest: it guided him to imagination, a light beyond Nature's light, yet bending back to Nature.

Thus Nature is not an obstruction, prison house, or delusive construct that must be deconstructed. The youngster's psyche is marked by scenes of both beauty and fear, by experiences of the countryside both real and ghostly. The "incumbent mystery" of soul and sense at once perplexes imagination and grounds it in common sights and sounds, in earthly manifestations that counterbalance revolutionary thoughts about a New Man "parted as by a gulph / From him who had been." The poet's subtle personifying of the spirit of lonely places always remained in the service of a return to nature. He wrote his autobiographical *Prelude* to affirm an early love of the Cumbrian countryside and refused to renounce a nativist and integral portion of his past in the name of revolutionary progress.

I should emphasize how much Bloom and I shared. Both had read Martin Buber's *I and Thou* and made significant use of it in dissertations that became our first books. The opening chapter of *The Unmediated Vision*, in proposing a cogito derived from Wordsworth, defined the basic intuition backing the poet's sense of identity via Buber's premise that relationship was not a matter of reasoning or logical systematization. A person, quite simply, found himself/herself "in relation." That relation, fundamental to a sense of existing "in this world which is the world of all of us," could be viewed as a variant of "I think, therefore I am"—namely, "This river: I am." A river, like the Wye, elemental at first, then embedded in associations, was typical of all distinct yet never disjunct natural objects (whether these were in the English countryside or the sublimer Alps). "And oh ye Fountains, Meadows, Hills, and Groves / Think not of any severing of our loves," the last stanza of the "Immortality Ode" begins.

It can be argued that "think" (later, "forbode") is an inadvertence or else a metaphorical transference from a quality in the human perceiver. But it could also be a sign that the poet refused to draw too sharp a line between object and subject, between "mute, insensate things" and the individual mind. This is explicit in "Tintern Abbey": what we "half-create, / And what perceive." There is a thought in things, even a "passion" in the forms of Nature, as Wordsworth proclaims elsewhere. The

"mighty world of eye and ear" passes through and sub-
sumes the whole soul and sensorium of a person: it is not
the inert subject of a thinking process, of an epistemologi-
cal inquiry. This perspective is not natural religion but
closer to what A. N. Whitehead will call "process
religion."

There was a difference, then, in what we took from
Buber. Bloom's first book, on Shelley's mythmaking, had
argued that the true poet enters an "I–Thou" rather than
"I–It" (reifying or neutral) relation, where the "Thou" is
mythic: an object—if an object at all—at the limit of
desire. What attracted me more was the concept of being
"in relation," and this is what I understood under the
name of Nature. Thus, at an earlier time, when I was still
unaware of Buber's thought, the fate of having been displaced opened onto a cheerful prospect during the years
in England. Out of doors, ruralized by a gentle countryside, I felt in touch with something universal and
unmediated.

To this day I remain astonished at the closeness of my
early thinking and that of Bloom. I say "early," for the
later Bloom is, as the expression goes, "something else."
A street fighter, as he often emphasized, brought up in a
tough section of New York City, he becomes, like his
Yahwe, a formidable man of war who does not cease
from mental fight against corruptions of the religious—as
well as academic—imagination. When, some fifty years
after our first encounter, I gave a series of lectures on
"Religion and Literature" at Notre Dame, I found, writing the talk on Shelley, that my first draft had unconsciously recreated that early affinity. Even the title of the
series, "Theopoesis," was in relation to our relation.

While Bloom, then, takes on Yahwe personally, still maintaining an I-Thou relation, and accusing Him, and not the Jewish people, of breaking the covenant, I continue to thread and unthread the tangled ties of poetry and divinity, the refusal of artists to yield ground to established religion.

Is there a contemporary reader who has as intimate a relation to poetry as Harold Bloom? At least to the poems he falls in love with? Laboriously I work from the outside in, intrigued by a poem's rich darkness, or, obversely, its "world of clear water, brilliant-edged" (Wallace Stevens). My conviction is that the poem's *mundo*—as Stevens, a shade too fondly, calls its imaginative world—will yield to the understanding despite its opaque, thing-like resistance ("No ideas but in things," as William Carlos Williams declared). But Bloom has the gift of intuiting a poem as if he had composed it. His "anxiety of influence" theory allows him to apply a mind as imprinted with poetry as that of the great poets themselves.

Each ambitious poet, according to Bloom, tries to measure up, to face an exceeding greatness. The critic seeks out the few truly strong minds that refuse to be overwhelmed. "Bloom's embrace of Western poetry since the Renaissance," I wrote in a review of *Anxiety* that tried to understand its gloomy picture of poetry's inevitable recession, "is a final desperate hug in the knowledge that there is nothing else." In a previous age, where branding took place through heraldic devices, Bloom's logo would have been: "This poet: I am." Or the exact contrary, which must also be endured: "This poet: I am—NOT." Bloom categorizes a sixfold of revisionary moves: ingenious allusions and devious imitations employed by belated poets who aspire to match a precursor. The ephebes deceive themselves in their desire for parity with a powerful father figure, and try to outwit that "eclipse" (as Emily Dickinson called her father) to make room for their own genius.

Blake too deceived himself this way, as Bloom later acknowledged. Blake thinks to revise Milton and even claims that the Hebrew Bible's prophetic and imaginative conceptions had been distorted and need recasting. By the time he writes *Anxiety*, Bloom has seen that Blake is indebted to a Pauline revisionism that recognizes the Bible as authoritative yet asserts of the Jews that their moral and theological understanding has been limited by God's will. The synagogue's vision is veiled. Christian revelation removes the veil. For Bloom, this claim of progress, of overgoing, is a paradigmatic reaction to the anxiety of influence. Thus it is the Old Testament, not the New, whose strength is the scandal.[14]

Who can escape the torment of creative jealousy? How few in each generation overcome it, especially among scholars and critics. They kill the thing they love, through pedantry, resentment, reductive judgments. Let us resolve, then, to tolerate the genius of others. As Blake wrote: "The most sublime act is to set another before you."

I feel embarrassed when, occasionally, younger colleagues, usually Jewish, address me as "my teacher." I realize this is fond and purely honorific, a secular version of "Rabbi." But it makes me aware of the fact that I have never thought of anyone in so personal a way as a role model. I did not wish to follow or have a

Georges Poulet.

following. The way Gide ends *Les nourritures terrestres*, "Nathaniel, jette mon livre!" delighted me. Yet here and there I did catch a glimpse of someone in our profession I would have liked to be closer to.

In December 1966, at the end of a visiting semester at the University of Zürich, where I substituted for Paul de Man, I met Georges Poulet, considered the chief of the "Geneva School" and an early influence on Hillis Miller (later my colleague at Yale). I had respected and enjoyed his books, but his person surprised me. He made me feel ashamed in a good way through his firmness, gentleness, directness, qualities somehow enhanced by his being so tall, as if that made me expect a more aggressive demeanor. "How he needs spiritual progeny! How he renounces that need!" I wrote in a note on our encounter. "As a man with an appointment glances at his watch, so here and there he seems to withdraw from his engaging warmth, his capacity to remain engaged, but these are purely natural moments of retreat, of an inward return, while giving the sense of hidden pain because of his habitual openness." It has rarely happened that my understanding of the work was so reborn by meeting the person. And it was "the person" one met in him, and so also in oneself, in conversation.

I remember he asked me what of American literary criticism would survive. Did anything make a difference, as Hazlitt's work for him? Could anyone stand with Auerbach, Spitzer, Curtius? I said that despite these names and others (he also was close to Albert Béguin and Marcel Raymond), I did not feel Europe was full of "génies critiques." Still, I agreed that little could compare with his Geneva friend Jean Starobinski's work on Rousseau, in the totality, clarity, subtleness, and respectfulness of its conception.

When he reproached me for starting too far outside (I had accused him of the opposite fault, of an overly easy spiritual intimacy with "his" authors), I agreed to the truth of his observation. But when conceding that in the Wordsworth book, at least, I ended up "inside," yet adding, citing the cry in one of the poems on Lucy's death, "And O, the difference to me!" that this deeply subjective confession was key, since, for Wordsworth, the "acte de conscience" was all, I asked him why all those genial European critics had never discussed Wordsworth in the Pouletian way? Indeed, why had *he* not written on Wordsworth? On Rousseau yes, always, but not Wordsworth. What he then said about "my" poet, linking him to the Augustinian tradition, was OK, but it left out the peculiar "détour vers soi-même" by way of Nature. Except for his essay on Maurice Guérin, Poulet did not consider that mediation. My good-bye was, "I have learnt from you," and he, "we have learnt that our friendship has grown and will continue to do so." I did not meet him again.

I. A. Richards, rejecting "History" as a university degree program, opined that "it [history] should never have happened." I too may have tried to escape from a history I was trying to ignore. Except for literature's own history. My initial response to the determinism or substantial influence of extraliterary mediations was confined to my specialty: "Toward Literary History" is the title of the final essay in *Beyond Formalism*. It expressed dissatisfaction with how historical knowledge was being applied to literature. "We are all disenchanted," I wrote, "with those picaresque adventures in pseudo-causality which go under the name of literary history, those handbooks with footnotes which claim to sing of the whole but load every rift with glue."

Formalism proved to be both hindrance and help. Did literary history have a distinct, internally evolving shape and progress, despite being entangled with social and political matters? How important was artistic greatness, how autonomous literary genius?

As Paul de Man emphasized, following the pedagogical practice of Reuben Brower at Harvard, these large questions led to the elementary one of what was involved in reading. Readers were to be made attentive enough and honest enough, as de Man wrote in *The Resistance to Theory*, "not to hide their non-understanding behind the screen of received ideas that often passes, in literary instruction, for humanistic knowledge." The history of literature was that of acts of reading bearing on and informed by literary works. I remained interested, at the same time, in canon formation, even if it betrayed an ideological element; also in the idea (never fully developed) that art could have a therapeutic influence on the individual's crises, and might not only communicate but help to think through rather than evade a conflicted state of mind. The aspect that was most appealing in Heidegger, therefore, was his concept of significant art as an event opening to the future, an event always still to be appropriated. Hölderlin had that effect on Heidegger, and Wordsworth proved to be my nemesis.

I find it hard to reconstitute my attitude toward literary history from the 1950s on. So much was happening. The older way of structuring literary history had employed concepts of tradition and revolt, or tradition and the individual talent.[15] But now the concept of secularization, active at least since Vico's time, engendered rich and fascinating patterns.[16] Literature was viewed as evolving into modernity by a humanistic appropriation of religious insights and themes. Or by their reappropriation, given the thesis of a self-alienation of the human source. "Thus men forgot that all deities reside in the human breast" (Blake, *The Marriage of Heaven and Hell*).

In the field of Romantic studies, narratives of this kind produced distinguished work into the 1970s, culminating in Meyer Abrams's *Natural Supernaturalism*. All the more so as Vico and his theory of the three ages (gods, heroes, men), each having its own language and *imaginaire*, became well known. Literary history, increasingly suspect because of its formalism—the separating out of the literary from sociopolitical and material contexts—saw a return of materialist perspectives stimulated by Vico's imaginative speculations as well as by Marx.

Erich Auerbach's soft, persuasive Marxism in *Mimesis* seemed to promise a way of integrating stylistic analysis and socioeconomic findings. (Auerbach was an early promoter and translator of Vico.) Raymond Williams, whose work on culture, literature, and society had become influential in the United Kingdom, was also an inspiration for the nascent cultural studies movement in the United States. In the 1970s, likewise, Fredric Jameson's *Marxism and Form* and *The Prison House of Language* returned strongly to material and philosophical reflections on art, including neglected German sources, while Paul de Man countered in his own way by rescuing the intricacies of (Romantic) irony from New Critical short-circuitings and made literary statements appear more philosophical in their self-reflective perspicacity than philosophical ones.

Formalism had a rough time, and not only because of increased demands all around for a grounding of art, exemplified by the New Historicism, in institutional types of history: of the church, stagecraft, media, trade. A rough time too, because formalism meant, as Susan Sontag realized, a breaking of forms, a radical experimentation with conventional narrative patterns, and so a challenge to sensibility itself. Her celebration (however qualified) of Alain Renais's film *Last Year at Marienbad* recognized the photo-stasis at the heart of the motion picture medium in a way that corroborated Eisenstein's emphasis on the generative principle of montage—a principle confirmed and expanded in *Marienbad*, where pieces of sound mix asymmetrically with the image track, as if piped in by memory. Stasis means ecstasy yet approaches the stillness of death. The paradox points away from ideology (Sontag was "Against Interpretation," but that slogan slanders the word) and toward a study of the defining limits of artistic media going back to Lessing's *Laocoon*. Saussure's semiology, too, as the study of sign systems in their inevitable social settings, applied an interesting mix of formalistic and material considerations.

Lévi-Strauss's structuralism was a sort of metaformalism. It demonstrated that myth and folklore acted in a paralogical way to mediate social rifts. Modern belief systems were no different. His insight questioned the Hegelian view of history as a mediatory process endowed with progressive momentum. Marx's powerful post-Hegelian tracts had already reenvisioned mediation in terms of material production. They framed history as the story of human liberty, one that overcomes the condition of alienated labor and the mind-forged manacles of enslaving religious strictures. But what did artistic rather than artisanal labor produce? What role, aside from propaganda, was played by literature, in particular, in the grand vista of liberation?

Given these pressures, it became difficult to think of art as an internal, self-modifying institution. The work-immanent perspective, at the same time, agreed with one of the pedagogical aims of the New Criticism—a movement that sought to prevent literary studies from being overwhelmed by ideological considerations (which did not mean its own motives were free of them). The New Critics also agreed, though in an unspecialized mode, with the science-oriented linguistic research of Roman Jakobson and the Moscow/Prague circle of formalists. (The latter's emphasis on aesthetic issues was, however, a deliberate indirection, an outflanking of oppressive political conditions in their homelands.) The literary theory emanating from this group, which began to be disseminated in Anglo-America in the 1930s, was not sufficiently known until after the Second World War. Then Wellek and Warren's *Theory of Literature* (1949) introduced an accommodated, if immensely learned, version of Continental formalism into the American university.

Things began to change rapidly only after Northrop Frye's *Anatomy of Criticism* (1957). It too is clearly indebted to Vico, positing a collective imagination that

The theory era and its return to Romanticism. Frye's evangel. Resistance to an age of prose. Pressure on the poet of the vernacular classics as well as the ancients. Walter Benjamin and the taint of culture. Going through formalism and beyond it with André Malraux and Kenneth Burke.

began with myth. In myth the actors are primarily gods; in the next stage, romance, gods and humans mingle; then a high mimetic mode appears, where humans are humans but include heroes close in capacity to the gods. After that we arrive at the low mimetic or completely realistic mode, and finally at an ironic phase, in which the protagonists are represented as all too human, so that readers may feel superior to them (that is, they are compelled to recognize an immanent frailty of their own). Frye, like Vico, envisaged a cyclical pattern, a return of the human imagination to the mythic and suprahuman—this was a version, shared by Yeats and Spengler, of history's recursion to an "organic" or religious period after a critical and skeptical age. But Spengler and Yeats anticipated a period of rebarbarization (already upon them) that would have to reinvigorate an overcivilized world.

The theory era in North America can be said to have begun in earnest with Frye's genially schematic book, and not only because it adapted Vico. Frye conveyed a sense of the liberal (and liberating) virtues of the study of art without worrying about the legitimacy of the canonical tradition, since he linked the latter to popular art through archetypal features.[17] Therefore what was conservative in Frye was also radical. For the *Anatomy*'s guiding paradigm bypassed formalist theories derived from linguistic, narratological, or semiotic concepts. It centered on the Bible as an inclusive ("encyclopedic") and still influential *literary* genre whose revolutionary potential was far from exhausted.

In a study of 1949, Frye had portrayed Blake's poetry as combating a variety of religions related to deism. They flourished in the Enlightenment and confined the Bible's visionary energies. But poetry fought to take back from divinity its own alienated legacy. Blake put himself behind Moses' famous reply to those who objected to the prophesying in the Israelite encampment: "Would to God that all the Lord's people were prophets" (Numbers 11). A wish like that was equally the inspiration of Frye's educationist, indeed evangelical conviction: literature, however sublime or class-bound, could be taught to everyone; it did not require an elite to be received. This proved to be an immensely seductive faith in view of the democratization of the American university gaining momentum in the 1960s.

The theory era's crucial turn toward the Romantics, whose religion of art was (with exceptions) populist rather than class-bound and exclusive, removed their low prestige and initiated a more complex view of poetry's situation in a modern industrialized society. Questions remained, of course. Did poetry in its fabulous, romance-oriented aspect spring from a popular and potentially revolutionary source, or was it an otiose remnant of aristocratic elites? Could the "visionary company"—a phrase migrating from Hart Crane to Harold Bloom's early, comprehensive book on the Romantic poets—survive? Because of the Enlightenment, was poetry other than social and satirical verse nearing its end?

The Romantics did not wish to give way to a demotic Age of Prose but understood the historical situation they were in. A reluctance to abandon traditional visionary forms was joined to hoping for a progressive literature that might bring about a second Renaissance (at once post-Enlightenment and post–French Revolution) without remnants of "superstition" (code for religious bigotry). It meant facing anew, especially in England and France, tradition's pressure—the pressure now coming not from canonical piety but, on the contrary, from acknowledging the near-transgressive linguistic fertility of a prior literary harvest.

This earlier flourishing of letters, the Renaissance, was of native vernacular as well as Classical inspiration. Although other European literatures participated, Britain's case was conspicuous. The canonical set of Spenser, Shakespeare, Donne, and Milton, in particular, made the prosaic era that followed seem poor—despite its development of an efficient prose, an expository and journalistic medium, and advances in science and technology. Both Walter Jackson Bate's pessimistic view of literary progression and the Freudian and more canny gloominess of Bloom's *Anxiety* recognized in this new, post-Classical embarrassment of riches an added, unconventional burden on aspiring writers, and so the issue was raised whether great art or the sublime "in the old sense" could survive.[18]

Further pressures, not only from, but on, the ideal of a sublime art, are still prevalent today, and flow from attempts to level high culture. The objective of study has shifted from literature as a relatively independent, inner-directed system toward its potential and often stymied contribution to social justice. Though Frye, Bate, and Bloom continued to acknowledge the struggles of genius against conformist social pressures, whether coming from above (state and church) or from below (the state of nature), many began to wonder whether any art-centered, grand narratives had validity, or if, as Walter Benjamin remarked in one of his last pronouncements, our historical experience and political disenchantment had reached the point where every artistic treasure, every cultural trophy, was tainted by being associated with the victors and the official history they sponsored. The victors' triumphal narratives covered oppositional cultural work with oblivion—until that could be exhumed by a revolutionary consciousness in solidarity with nameless or neglected authors.[19]

Was I already, then, an Ancient, facing avant-garde Moderns whose values were no longer influenced by the great art of the past? Or was an alternate history under construction, expanded by anthropological insight and ideals of social restitution?

For a time, André Malraux's wide-angle humanism, encompassing Eastern as well as Western paintings and sculptures, was a comfort: his concept of a museum without walls (enabled by photography) and his luxurious pictorial illustration of the thesis that the gods could retain their sublimity—though only as works of art. Malraux, whose formalism in art was as revolutionary as his early politics, still promoted the genius idea and the individual artist's creative struggle with past masters. More positive than Benjamin, he saw technologies of reproduction saving the aura of the greatest producers by ushering in a humanistic metamorphosis rather than bringing about a celluloid diminishment.[20]

Kenneth Burke too wished to retain an emphasis on the formalism of art. Statements about a poem's subject or content, he remarks in *The Philosophy of Literary Form*, are also statements about its form. I want to pay homage to this extreme and genial bricoleur who took on a wide variety of philosophic, psychological, and sociological challenges. More mutable, eclectic, and outrageous than Frye, but also therefore less influential, he managed to keep his eye firmly on the formal properties of art. At the same time, a type of analysis he called "socioanagogic" helped him to honor "the ways in which things of the senses are secretly emblematic of motives in the social order" (preface to the second edition of *Counter-Statement*, his earliest book of literary-critical essays). Even if he shifts emphasis from book to book and tries out various cryptological unmaskings influenced by both Freud and an anthropological, post-Frazer sense of the trace in ancient Greek drama of a lost religious ritual, his specific literary readings are among the most acute as well as daring. They do not add up to one grand system, despite his terminological exertions, yet they recall the need to deal with "discordant voices arising out of many systems" (*Counter-Statement*).

The motto he adopted, "Toward a purification of war," catches his situation as a writer maturing in the between-wars era, particularly an admittedly obsessive fascination with the purgative function of art, its debunking of euphemisms on the one hand and its working through of a cacophony of voices on the other. One is struck, as well, by Burke's rhetorical and dramatistic emphasis on "strategies," which anticipates the emphasis on performance in contemporary media studies. He stands close to Hui-zinga, whose *Homo Ludens*, also under the pressure of the 1930s, made clear how conflict resolution depended on the same inventiveness that art sponsors and displays.

Valéry, another formalist thinker of that time, remarked ironically: "L'abîme de l'histoire est assez grand pour tout le monde" ("the abyss of history is big enough for everyone, for the entire world"). He was reacting to the continued rise of democratic and egalitar-ian ideals. They could even embrace (but this quirky anal-ogy is my own) "Rudolph, the red-nosed reindeer." A candy-colored Christmas song, it celebrates the fact that Rudolph, having been ostracized, but then achieving fame when chosen to be Santa's helper, was able to "go down in history."

The formalism I retained expressed a hope that poetry mattered as well as history, that there would be some exit from history's serial bloodiness back to the more durable republic of the arts. So far I have described the intellectual solicitations all around me from the 1950s on. Now I should render as faithful a picture as possible of how my own thinking fared after the publication of *Wordsworth's Poetry*.

I never got to write a "new" literary history. Fragments, yes; studies of how most Romantics and pre-Romantics envisioned their historical situation *as poets*. How they fought to preserve the Romance heritage—its thesaurus of old stories and fantasies—against the scientifically cor-rect and merciless light of the Enlightenment. Visionary histories arose to protect art from a progress denied to it, a progress dooming it as a relic of a primitive mentality.

These counterhistories were projected by artists who felt deeply the precarious status of poetry (of Poesy, the artistic imagination, *Dichtung*) in their society. Even if literature simply recovered lost or suppressed voices, if it inspired a "Philomela project," that was something.

The ballad revival, sweeping over Europe in the period usually characterized as Romantic, was more than antiquarian and nationalistic. It wished to enrich both oral and written literature. What role can creative writers play in a needy time, Hölderlin had asked. What are literary critics for, I asked myself, if they do not at once revive traditional and respect unusual voices?

At times, the historical consciousness, as it caught up with me, demanded a more forceful intervention. If not that of a political activist, then of a satirist, like Karl Kraus in *Die Fackel* or Pope in *The Dunciad*, or else the fecund Victor Hugo's historical and mythographic *Légende des Siècles*. Into my sixties I kept, nevertheless, to a subprophetic—scholarly and essayistic—mode, as in *Minor Prophecies* (1991). I praised the genre of the essay as a nondeclamatory, low-key engagement in cultural affairs. While extending to the domain of the essayist Edmund Spenser's dictum that poets should have the kingdom of their language, I was wary of a not-quite-dispelled nightmare: the inflated and seductive rhetoric aiming at an *Aufbruch* or *renascimento*, a revivalist politics of education joined to cultural prediction and predication. I found myself in a bind: on the one hand, regretting the repressive effect on imaginative thought coming from the English Enlightenment's fear of religious "enthusiasm"—a fear whose traces could still be discerned in the establishment criticism of my time—yet, on the other, totally approving of that caution in the political sphere.

Even as I write, scholarly voices approach ideological pathos again. They are formidably erudite, swelling a conservative revolution that can denounce the "pretentious nihilism," "the saturnalia of post-structural and deconstructionist literary theories."[21] I sense philology becoming a theology once more, close to Heidegger's quasi-religious apotheosis of pre-Socratic fragments and certain major German poems. In Germany today, with more fidelity to Greek or Latin texts than Heidegger's depth-exegeses, or by a sophisticated evocation of ancient Egypt as well as Greece, committed cultural writers speculate on what went wrong with monotheistic religion, in particular the political theologies it is said to have fostered. The revival elsewhere in Europe of an interest in theology by thinkers who claim a very mixed heritage—including materialism, atheism, and an appreciation of Walter Benjamin's recuperation of the messianic impulse in Marxism—has led to a return to Paul as the apostle of a universalism that might save us from both ethnic particularism and too abstract a globalism.[22] Whether fighting to remove historical blinkers or lured by the prestige of origins, such revisionary readings of ancient texts are corrective and fruitful—as long as the battle, which always at first targets public education, does not regress to a Mao-type cultural revolution and a new ideological justification of the God—the political theology—that failed.

It is instructive to read again, at present, Max Weber's "Scholarship [*Wissenschaft*] as Vocation." Weber issued an eloquent warning toward the end of the First World War against the revival of messianic politics. Yet even he cannot avoid the charged word "Schicksal" (destiny or fate) in the attempt to define his profession ("Beruf") as a calling ("Ruf"). He urged scholars to accept modern realities, the disenchantment of the world together with the rationalizing and intellectualizing drive that had resulted in a withdrawal from the public sphere of values previously held to be sublime. He cautioned those who could not tolerate the continued absence of prophet or messianic leader, asking them to give up seeking mystical political unions or communions. With barely concealed scorn he pressed them to accept the modern situation, or, if they could not, then to retreat into the arms of the ancient churches—but quietly, without staging a public scandal ("Renegatenreklame"). Compared to Weber's clarity of analysis and voice, *Minor Prophecies*, subtitled *The Literary Essay in the Culture Wars*, strikes me today as notes emitted in the attempt to tune a dissonant instrument—whose tuning is the tune that is left.

Of the two paths I now followed, one was conventionally academic, the other more risky. The first had—at last—a combative as well as irenic component. I will try and explain it before describing the second, more disturbing and initially extra-academic path.

Could I mediate between literary criticism and society's careless, even contemptuous attitude toward literary academics, as well as between Anglo-America and continental Europe? These aims mingle in *Criticism in the Wilderness* (published in 1980, ten years after *Beyond Formalism*). Together with an earlier collection, *The Fate of Reading* (1976), *Wilderness* tried to broaden the literary-critical spectrum. It charged, "We have caused our own impotence by allowing the concept of practical criticism to reduce to its lowest social or utilitarian value." Impressed at the 1978 English Institute sessions by René Girard and Stephen Greenblatt, whose papers raised religious and anthropological issues (Girard) and political and postcolonial ones (Greenblatt), I noted in a diary: "What 'criticism of life' can be laid hold of today. . . . We have killed off the preacher in the teacher, and the teacher has become the marginal man, the idiot questioner in the spectator sport of criticism. Can practical criticism become practical once more in the strongest sense of that word?"

Redefining practical criticism. Theory's dependence on a text-milieu. The impact of popular culture in Anglo-America. The messy hinterland of art. Culture no longer the Arnoldian study of perfection.

Yet I rarely invoked the aid of specific social, economic, or large-scale political theories. Instead, my essays looked for reform from within. They emphasized what difference changes in a consecrated text-milieu (a word preferable to "canon") might make to the formulation of literary theory. Add Racine, or Hölderlin, or Paul, or Hegel, or Marx, or Pushkin, or Bialik, or even a self-styled *"aliéné authentique"* like Artaud to the reading list of the Anglo-American syllabus—and, to be even-handed, augment the French curriculum by Spenser, or Jonathan Edwards, or Wordsworth, or Melville, or a "mad" genius like Christopher Smart—and theory too changes. This even without considering the possible impact of non-European literatures.

Roland Barthes and later the American New Historicism also expand the text-milieu, though by means of a different strategy. The energy of their theories no longer depends exclusively on consecrated authors but includes popular culture, women writers, and minor (minority) literature considered as a subversive vernacular, a *vox populi*. This produces a curriculum but hardly a canon. Culture here is not Arnold's "study of perfection." It temporizes and allows theory to liberate criticism so that the latter can gauge the expressive potential of texts from anywhere in the world, which also implies finding a way to honor oral traditions, ancient or contemporary.

One result is that contemporary-culture critics have almost abandoned the attempt to judge mass culture. The polemic of an F. R. Leavis or the Frankfurt School seems at once just and hysterical. "Just"—because, as a recent reviewer of pop affairs complained, there is now a large body of songs for which getting out of bed in the morning, especially when depressed, is as momentous as Moses dividing the Red Sea.

If popular culture, nevertheless, can be inspiring, despite, recently, its in-your-face vulgarity, its histrionic, commercially rapacious, and self-consuming character, this is because it replenishes at times not only the energies of political protest but also lasting works of art. So Shakespeare's mix of high and low, courtier and clown, marks forever the English literary tradition and is admired almost everywhere—except by Tolstoian religious purists and French neoclassicists. The popular romances (lovingly spoofed by Cervantes), the ballad revival from Bishop Percy's collection, so influential for the Romantics, to that of Harry Smith's in the 1950s and its impact on Bob Dylan and Joan Baez (even if tumbling today from elite nineteenth-century musical settings to crotch-clutching performers), Brecht and Weill's *Three-penny Opera*, Bakhtin's understanding of the carnival character of writers like Rabelais, E. P. Thompson's mining of the literature of Dissent and radical politics in the English seventeenth and eighteenth centuries, Robert Darnton's recovery of local turmoil anticipating the French Revolution, and rare, poignant testimonial remnants of the daily life and suffering of Afro-American slaves—these too expand our awareness of the explosive hinterland of art. Similarly, Lévi-Strauss's sophisticated analysis transformed orally transmitted stories and what had been thought of as primitive myths into texts with an intelligible structure.

By stressing theory's text-dependence I was seeking to acknowledge its hidden parochialism and residual dogmatic bent, yet also shielding it from accusations that it corroded deep-seated national customs instead of sustaining local or traditionary feeding sources. The tense relation of local to global, so conspicuous at the present time, has been surfacing since an ethos of "local attachment" arose in the latter part of the eighteenth century. The emphasis on spirit of place was not entirely retro and sentimental but contained an instinctive reaction to a growing cosmopolitan trend. Matthew Arnold eventually fused commentary's judicial function, essentially conservative (defensive of parochial values), with the circulation of new ideas that might have a creative effect without setting off panic alarms about Jacobin disorders.

Criticism in the Wilderness, subtitled *The Study of Literature Today*, attempted to revise and revive Arnold's legacy. It attacked the reduced and routinized use made of

Saving Arnold's
legacy from the
New Criticism.
The Concordat
between
creative and
critical. Literary
criticism as a
literary genre.
Roland Barthes's
example. The
attraction of
minor genres.

him in Anglo-American circles and apposed a
Continental model of literary reflection inspired
by (and sometimes inspiring) linguistics, philosophy, hermeneutics, and other disciplines. I
argued that the New Criticism, influential from
the 1930s into the 1960s, had simplified the
Arnoldian Concordat between creative and
critical.

Following T. S. Eliot, the New Critics insisted
that while even lyric poetry should be tough and
self-aware, criticism itself was not creative.
Reluctant to acknowledge the innovative reach
of the critical spirit, or fearing that its growth would subvert creativity, they curtailed criticism's role. Arnold,
however, had assigned an essential function to the critical
sphere, that of undoing English philistinism, chauvinism,
etc., so that a broadened knowledge, a circulation of
ideas, could bring about a new kind of literature, intellectual as well as imaginative.

The literature Arnold foresaw was already in place: it
was the literature of criticism. By asserting that criticism
could not be creative, Eliot implicitly condemned it to an
auxiliary and entirely dependent role. From my perspective, literary commentary at its best *is* literature, or a
genre (if minor and often rambunctious) within the literary domain, rather than condemned to look in from the
cold. The literary-critical essay's assimilated learning can
foster and disseminate ideas; moreover, its language
could be inventive, not only technical, as Barthes demonstrated ingeniously by recycling specialized terms of semiotics to augment words of love in his *A Lover's
Discourse.*

The flak that came my way, the charges of self-promotion and puffing my profession, can be imagined. That my argument served a new and stronger alliance of critical prose and major literary works was overlooked. Exiled to the proverbial desert isle, I would have gladly left behind most literary criticism for the "majors." My actual practice was clearly devoted to a literature that enriched both the imagination and the language.

Still, it is true (my love of movies aside, especially those combining popular content with a sophisticated technique) that I am attracted to minor genres, to literary forms with a small footprint and large resonance. I shy from anatomizing authors whose greatness depends on elements that seem to exceed their diction. I am reluctant to analyze them, as if my tendency for getting caught up by words within words, by textures of speech, would become, when applied to larger genres, a kind of pedantry or *lèse majesté*. I recognize the importance of big novelistic productions but find it difficult to avoid, on the one hand, collapsing them into expressive plot structures, and, on the other, into a compact display of the potential precision and micromegas power of language. I realize that novel and drama reveal the masks and personae we inhabit, interchange, and wish to enjoy, even though we are often trapped by them. Yet an antitheatrical prejudice usually gets the better of me. My intellectualizing side, moreover, always wants to prevail, so I break the hypnotic spell or am sidetracked by a work's episodic aspects, by bravura effects that illuminate even B-grade movies and gimmicky plots. I cannot rule out that this penchant to use smaller things to hint at greater ones may seek to bypass value judgments and suggests a failure of nerve related to my distaste for polemics. When

I do venture a largish generalization, I like to make sure it is a noncoercive emanation of a delight in words and perennial forms. I rehearse how these are refigured or even transfigured, how they "adorn," as Milton would say, English, the mother tongue.

The contemporary linguistic turn. *Glas* and the two-columned merging of philosophical and literary commentary. Derrida's *paranomasia* ("epiphony") and political as well as linguistic boundary crossing. Against the purity-perplex. The missing history of remainders, of "trash." *Saving the Text* and my search for a theory of the praxis of close reading.

English, and other national vernaculars: a linguistic turn had occurred in the Renaissance through verbal riches gradually acquired yet exploding in the genius of the great writers of the period. Latin, as father tongue, had given way to multiple Romance mother tongues close to everyday speech. (Latin continued to be cultivated as the shared language of scholarly and philosophical writing.) Although not directly dependent on Latin's linguistic metamorphosis, English benefited from an infusion of the Romance heritage through the Norman influence. In Europe, thus, a variety of national literatures emerged, enriched by a treasury of tropes translated from the revived classics as well as the Latin Middle Ages.

Philology also, no longer engendering endless glosses upon glosses in the service of religious exegesis, began to flourish by authenticating texts through careful standards of editing, and made that an integral part of interpretation. Combining linguistic and literary perspectives also today, four centuries later, philology does not forget the recovery work of the original group of scholars called humanists.

But the linguistic turn of our time, which still needs clearer definition, takes on Babel itself, as if languages had an underlying, universal structure.[23] Markedly from Mallarmé on, it skirts both a mystical semiotics and depth psychology, in addition to astringent modes of logical analysis by Wittgenstein and related thinkers. This new linguistic turn is not only intensely introspective but also accompanied by the extraversions of theory. Today, therefore, we cannot neglect the fact that language is indefeasibly the object as well as vehicle of thought, whether in commentary or fiction.

Enter Jacques Derrida. Soon after it was published in 1974, I recognized in *Glas* a pivotal work of both philosophical criticism and art. *Glas* blended commentary on Hegel, in one column of a vertically divided page, with commentary on Jean Genet in a facing column. The Romantic dream of *Symphilosophieren*, first conceived in the Germany of the 1790s, and which pointed to a symbiosis of philosophy and art, had finally come to fruition.

Derrida's oversize book of peculiar juxtapositions is a wondrous expansion of the linguistic turn. Its every line is marked by a tireless semiotic, phonemic, and literary scrutiny. Derrida could already have said what he told the *Le Monde* interviewer two months before his death: "To leave a mark on the history of the French language, that is what interests me."[24]

Conscious, also, of the *carré* as the right-angled container or "encadrement" that segments writing's flow, Derrida breaks out of the literary equivalent of the picture frame. Each column has its own continuity but is not impermeable to oblique interconnections. ("La chose est oblique," he avers, mixing colloquial and metaphysical.)

This generates a multidirectional kind of reading and a sense that the delimited verbal and semantic space, the bookishness of the book, can barely encompass (if at all) such border crossings.

Linguistic process, moreover, by potentially undermining strict borderlines, accrues political connotations. Those borders, inclusive of nation as well as individual identity construction, have proved to be especially changeable in Central and Eastern Europe.[25] At the cultural level, moreover, *Glas* is something of a digest of France's philosophical debt to Germany as well as French developments between the wars; it transcends the bloody Franco-German conflicts that had proved how divisive and destructive nationalized concepts of culture could be.

We are always kept aware of the linguistic turn as it reduces the distinction between the language of the object of inquiry and a metalanguage seeking to make statements about that object. Such a redoubled language consciousness also tends to blur the boundary between philosophical and literary commentary.

A danger resulting from this is that critical prose becomes more difficult and involuted, without offering the compensating pleasures of fiction. Derrida declines to push anything over the margin, to leave it out or unattended: the direction of his thought flow, more mournful than manic, barely emerges at times from merging with his subject. It avoids the very edge or boundary it is always seeking.

Besides, how can commentators introduce suspense into their prose, or the interplay of persons engaged in a dramatic action? Suspension of disbelief, essential to the success of imaginative literature, does not occur in commentary. When something like it is tried, with critics pretending to believe an interpretation before demolishing it, the effort is painfully artificial. It rarely works even for authors who stage dialogues. The best a commentator can do is to argue against a received opinion so forcefully that readers are bound to suspend their previous belief.

The linguistic turn has increased attentiveness to language as a marvelous instrument.[26] Wittgenstein, in the *Tractatus*, substitutes wonder at the existence of language for the metaphysical astonishment that "there is something rather than nothing," the sentiment that so often jumpstarts philosophical inquiry. Kenneth Burke emphasizes that words about words ("logology") do not distract from worldly matters but are an implicate of every discursive engagement. Bakhtin's theory of dialogism contains a dramatic perspective on the turbulent language-milieu in which writers try, consciously or unconsciously, to maneuver. His concept of the polyphonic or dialogic imagination tells us that the word "cannot fail to brush up against thousands of living dialogic threads." It is entangled in a "tension-filled environment of alien words, value judgments and accents, weaves in and out of complex relationships"[27] as it breaks through to its own meaning.

Bakhtin speaks mainly about the novel, but the borderlines of that literary genre are elastic. If what remains of Bakhtin's philological rather than linguistic focus has made the gulf between general and specialist reader even less bridgeable than before, a nonhierarchic separation of styles by critical genre may be the only solution. Ambidextrous critics can make a distinction, with an eye on their audience, between the "indefinite" article (book review or other nonfiction prose in the friendship style of what used to be called the familiar essay) and the highly specialized, "definite" article.

Glas begins notoriously by "joycing" the name Hegel into *aigle*, dropping an H that is usually not pronounced in French. This sort of homonymic punning continues throughout, as does the permutation of the *gl* sound, close to the throat. It haunts, in Derrida's "phonogrammatic" verbal play, a large array of words, including the series *glas, glace, glaïeul, angle, sigle, seigle, aigle, gel,* and *glu*. I confess that at the time of my engagement with *Glas* I was working on the greatest English extracanonical poet, Christopher Smart, and might have imitated *Glas* by a juxtaposition that would have replaced Hegel with Derrida and Genet with Smart or Joyce.

Derrida's overdeterminations, often as ingenious as those of Smart and Joyce, but reminiscent also of dada and surrealist experiments—think of Duchamp's feminine alter ego, "Rose Sélavy," and Denos's versionings[28]—produce an excess, an "epiphony" at once enriching, playful, and disconcerting. The eagle points to an imperial heraldic emblem associated with Hegel's attempt at philosophic mastery, here subverted by the hazards, the *coup de dés(rrida)*, of linguistic process. That process, while dividing or combining sounds to become words, accepts no absolute boundary, including that which separates philosophy and literature.

By a further doubling, the eagle (that double-headed monstrosity serving as the ensign of Austro-Hungary) presides not only over the dual columns of *Glas* but, as an animalistic trumping of Genet's flower name, is the emblem of John the Evangelist. Jean Genet's life project, its acute gender ambivalence fixated on mother and mother tongue, is transvalued as the sacred, not just sacrilegious, gospel of a contemporary "Saint Jean." That title had already been bestowed on Genet by Jean-Paul Sartre's humongous biography of 1952.

Though *Saving the Text* (1981), written at the same time as *Criticism in the Wilderness*, was mainly devoted to the significance of *Glas* for Anglo-American readers, I had often to insist that there was life before Derrida. I was never a boa-deconstructor; Derrida's importance for me came from the inventive genius of a commentary that revealed him to be a close reader, a literature-reading philosopher, in fact—nowadays an endangered species. In the 1950s, I had seized on the example of Maurice Blanchot, dubbing him a "philosopher-novelist." Sartre's literary criticism also impressed me, and I continue to admire the willingness of French intellectuals, after two deadly conflicts fought in good part on French soil, to engage with German philosophical thought, to stand in a critical relation to it, and even, as in Blanchot's *récits*, to create a nearly new mode of fiction.[29]

What I lacked, and Derrida seemed to promise, was a theory to back up the more-than-close reading I had been practicing and which I now directed at his own text. By making the linguistic turn a turn into deconstruction, Derrida at once critiqued and preserved the idea of Europe, refusing to see Europe mainly as a crime scene because of two world wars, colonialism, and the Holocaust. He continued to value a culture that, since the

Enlightenment, had exercised an "autocritique en permanence."[30]

Moreover, despite his attack on an essentialist type of reading he named "logocentric," Derrida was also preserving, or, as I put it, saving, the canonical texts. He made their previously neglected, marginalized, and even routinized features light up, so that, as in the most daring of religious commentaries, nothing might be overlooked. His "grammatological" perspective—which distinguished between writing as *écriture* and its closure (enclosure) in the form of The Book (he saves texts from their book misfortune, to paraphrase Levinas)—complicated the mimetic referentiality of those texts and removed the fear of an interpretive and intertextual infinitizing that had been restricted to the word-world of sacred Scripture.

His oft-cited statement that there is nothing outside the text does not imply a flight from reality into pantextualism: its scandal is simply that it restates the wondrousness of writing. The limits of textual interpretation are the limits of the reader; it is we who stabilize the meaning of significant works by following their formal solicitation or imposing a closure of our own. Thinking, as it questions itself, as it engages with and reflects on its medium, finds only provisional boundaries between a particular work (*ergon*) and what is textually offside or outside that work (*parergon*).

Was I drawn to Derrida because I aspired to a greater measure of philosophical dignity? Yes. That aspiration had also attracted me to Heidegger. But something unexpected happened. *Glas*, as a "discours de la folie" nourished by a humor resembling a melancholy milk (Thomas Gray, a learned eighteenth-century poet, coined the term "leucocholy"), took its toll and convinced me of the fool-ishness of that ambition. For it confirmed that the ideal of totality—embodied by a magisterial book, or a Hegelian type of philosophy and worldview, or any purity-per-plex motivating a universal language, or a complete harmony between theory and practice—was not only impossible to achieve but also dangerous. Dangerous because it denied that something was always left over or out, treated as dirt, excess, irrelevant texture.

So we need a history of trash, precisely of things deval-ued, marginalized, discarded. Consigned to dump rather than archive. They include mad or worn-out coinages that even literature has difficulty absorbing. We have begun to scavenge them, and we hope for an alchemy, a philosopher's stone, to turn trash into treasure, shit into gold. Are we in the last gasp of a museal culture, a stage of "archive fever" beyond the restoration of ruins? But what if everything becomes a collectible? I leave that to your (or DeLillo's) imagination. Capitalism certainly does not help, either from the side of planned obsolescence or of speculators who buy up every artifact that gambles on the value of trash. The junkyard turns operatic.

Hegel in the *Phenomenology* almost succeeds in over-coming the fact that the surplus threatens to turn into a clogging waste. He fashions a history practically without names. His dialectic ingeniously recycles the "dust heap" of ideological positions. So too, Wallace Stevens in "Man on the Dump" seems almost fond of the accumulated poetic detritus from which "the the" must emerge. We witness the end of a pure poetry tradition.

Glas linguistically scatters (compare the "petits carrés" in the opening of Derrida's Genet column)[31] identity markers in ways that inscribe their purging. This playful onomatoclasm is not a symptom of a capitalistic economy's so-called creative destruction. It exposes, rather, all monumentalizing and purity ideals influencing language ideology, genre and gender delimitations, and the call in political religions for ethnic or national purification. Derrida does not want his book, or Book-to-Come, to be a massive *tombeau*, a series of proper names gracing their narcissistic entombment in a monumental history.[32] Whatever history may be, literature is not a mausoleum. He joins Georges Bataille in acknowledging a heterology of remainders ("le reste").

Among these remainders are intellectual aporias but also the inner experience of (socially) unavowable ecstasies. Some are sexual, some religious, some both. They shock and shame, yet with a rebound similar to what, according to Kant, is a dialectical effect of "the sublime" that strengthens the humbled ego once more. In the public sphere, however, the sublime rebound from a collective humiliation, or what is taken to be such, can detonate a manic catharsis, the frenzy of extreme nationalism.

Derrida's paranomasia is directed also against himself. Therefore, in signing off, he omits his own name and ends *Glas* with: "le débris de."

I felt personally close to Derrida, admiring his dedication to students and younger faculty at Yale and his quiet reserves of affection. He valued friendship even as he examined and elaborated the concept. His main intellectual companions at Yale were Paul de Man and Hillis Miller. His loyalty to de Man, after the revelation of the latter's wartime journalism, was unwavering, and he may not have entirely forgiven me for questioning, during an otherwise amiable conversation at lunch in a favorite Paris hotel, the *Lucrèce* (where, after the war, the survivors of the Nazi camps had been temporarily lodged), the type of defense he launched in a famous *Critical Inquiry* article.

At that time he did not speak or write much about his own background. But I recall a Passover Meal at our home where he surprised us by intimating it was the first Seder he had celebrated since Algeria, and he described his father's demeanor, the way he presided and distributed the unleavened bread.

During the time of Derrida's visit, my friendship with Paul de Man deepened. He had joined the Yale faculty in 1970. It was shortly after de Man's arrival and until a year or so after his death in 1983 that Derrida taught at Yale each year for six weeks, sponsored by the department of comparative literature rather than philosophy. De Man and I first became friends when he invited me to join him at Cornell in 1965 to establish its comparative literature program and spell him at the University of Zürich, where he held an associate professorship.

Our cooperation at Cornell and Yale was based on a shared love for literature that welcomed rather than resisted the cultivation of metalanguages drawn from linguistics, rhetoric, philosophy, semiotics. The emphasis was on interpretation theory and practice. We knew that the intellectual ante had to be raised, and if that meant some terminological adventures, so be it. The emphasis on literature's linguistic and rhetorical riches was meant to encourage, as in Derrida, a border-crossing and transnational perspective at a time in which, as Danilo Kiš remarked, culture politics (mainly though not exclusively in Eastern Europe) were intent on limiting the writer's choice to "recommending ideological pollution in place of Coca-Cola Bottles." In the American university, the "comparative" in comparative literature meant freedom from too narrow a canon based on national literature departments as from an increasingly unreflective use of New Critical terms.

Later I realized that both de Man and I had been impressed by Husserl's "Philosophy as a Rigorous System of Knowledge." It contained the declaration that great names should not dazzle. "For the philosopher who is truly without prejudice," Husserl wrote, "it is all the same whether an affirmation stems from Kant or Aquinas, from Darwin or Aristotle, from Helmholz or Paracelsus." Yet de Man's remarks in *Blindness and Insight* pointed to Husserl's unquestioned privileging of a Hellenistic European consciousness even while he was promoting philosophy as a relentless critique. "Why," de Man writes, "this geographical expansion [of a universalistic, enlightened, and rigorous philosophy] should have chosen to stop, once and forever, at the Atlantic Ocean and the Caucasus, Husserl does not say."

Husserl, however insightful, seemed blind to the fact that his ideal, while implying a peaceful rather than militant concept of culture, continued to sponsor a mystified anthropology that Claude Lévi-Strauss, cited by de Man, helped to dispel. De Man accepts, however, that both philosophy and literary study are necessary for a prolegomenal critique of the human sciences.

There was something permanently quizzical about de Man. I became very fond of his demeanor: those eyes that looked at you acutely, steadfastly, yet always with a smile, and that slightly hunched form, as if weighed down by an Old World knowledge. He could be, as every one knew, quietly devastating in his comments at public lectures and conferences. Even privately he claimed to know "de trut." I did not always escape his suspicion that a personal vanity was at play. Discussing with him rather passionately some discovery I thought I had made in Wordsworth, he called it with his usual smile a "trouvaille" and passed on.

At Yale we organized and team taught an undergraduate core course in a new literature major on "Reading and Rhetorical Structure." It included poetry and fiction but extended our respective ways of reading to philosophy and other kinds of prose. Many thought I was practicing deconstruction without a license.

From my perspective, criticism, as reading to the second power, did not have to conflict with pleasures of the text. It was not the idea of the course to apply theory as a mode of "mastering" or "resolving" complex verbal artifacts or even to gain a disciplined distance from them in order to make some enlarged worldly statement. I preferred to draw a verbal artifact named "theory" from our readings and present it as an active mode of contemplation feeding back into the text. If philosophy and literature had an affinity rather than being adversaries, this would emerge from the possibility de Man and I were jointly exploring. His analytic acumen, of course, when it came specifically to philosophic texts, left me far behind.

De Man's illness showed itself in the summer of 1982, during the session at Northwestern of the School of Criticism and Theory. My wife and I noticed he was less sociable than usual. He responded to our concern by insisting nothing was wrong: his stomach was uneasy, he was used to that, the trouble would go away as it always did by drinking milk. Little over a week into the session his skin took on a yellowish tinge. Since he would do nothing about it, we made a doctor's appointment for him; the doctor immediately sent him back to New Haven for a complete examination. An "unreferenced" tumor was diagnosed. It was putting pressure on his liver and was too close to be removed. Paul continued to hold a seminar from his house and roused himself when visitors or students came, showing a disposition his wife characterized as that of "an old war-horse." He died toward the end of 1983.

Four years after de Man's death, the news broke of his journalism during the Nazi occupation of Belgium. It showed him sympathetic to Flemish national aspirations and deceived by the cultural policy of the occupier. Nazi policy at first co-opted the Idea of Europe, flattering populations in Western Europe by pretending to befriend and even preserve their national traditions under German protection. That helped to lessen resistance movements and released an occupying force to serve eventually on the Eastern front.

De Man's reviews of mediocre books in the major Belgian newspaper *Le Soir*, many from a Nazi-promoted "Otto list" (named after the regime's ambassador in France), also betrays symptoms of resentment at France's cultural hegemony. But his worst compromise was to contribute an essay to a special (also especially vicious) page devoted to antisemitic propaganda in that paper. He denied that Jews had exerted a strong influence on European culture, stating that it was healthy enough to resist foreign intrusions including the *ingérence sémite*. Were the Jews, he wrote, to be sent to a "colony" isolated from Europe it would make no difference to literature.[33] It is not difficult to discern behind the suave language a coarse ideology.

Yet I considered the reaction of the mass media in the States historically naive and exploitative. The "American Adam," as R. W. B. Lewis had dubbed a cultivated ignorance of historical precedent, was much in evidence. The journalists—but also a number of my fellow academics—did not know and did not bother to find out about the persistent undercurrent of antisemitism in European intellectual circles. Though often casual, it could turn into something as programmed and blatant as Charles Maurras's "antisémitisme d'état."

The historical fact does not excuse de Man's participation, even though it happened, nontrivially, only this one time. The pain is not lessened by pointing out that his cultural antisemitism in the *Le Soir* article reflected widespread assumptions that made Nazi policy toward the Jews acceptable also among intellectuals. It brings up the question of a failure, even betrayal, on their part, and the hollowness of their claim to be the conscience of Europe's cultured classes. This aspect of de Man's journalism should have led to a deeper kind of sociological inquiry.

Concerning de Man himself, no evidence was later found that his *antisémitisme de plume* carried over into personal relations. Indeed, on that level, there is evidence to the contrary. Yet unable to defeat deconstruction intellectually, its American opponents used the Holocaust cudgel against it. Deconstruction was condemned as, somehow, the extension of a fascistic mindset.

I too had been in error, however. Not about de Man's intelligence, already clear in his youthful ability to write these doubtful reviews at twenty-one, without compromising entirely, except for the *Le Soir* piece already mentioned, his literary integrity. Nor wrong about the consistency with which he later pulled down the vanity of philosophy by showing the dependence of its supposedly rigorous language on figurative and other literary devices. But mistaken about the image I held of him: it had not entered my mind that he might have passed through a phase of collaboration. I had always thought of him as an inner émigré, or, like myself, a refugee from Europe.

How did this confusion come about? The immediate reason was de Man's closeness to Derrida. Their mutual respect impeded any suspicion that de Man during the war might have been different from the de Man we knew. Both de Man and Derrida were of a recognizable European mold, philosophical minds interested in cultural matters and with a penchant for works of art and especially literature. But the main reason for my mistake was a reluctance, rather common at the time, for bringing one's personal background into the field of study.

De Man was not always averse to conveying gossip or making sharp characterizations of other scholars, but he never volunteered any information on his previous life, either in what he wrote or in social situations; nor did he ask about my own past. I hesitated to press him, and the occasions on which I did produced evasive answers. (Hart-man: "Paul, your bibliography lists no significant essay before 1953. Surely you published something before that date." De Man: "Nothing but journalism.") The impersonality fostered as a standard Modernist value in art was also a principle of academic decorum. It is totally reversed by the proliferation of memoirs surrounding us today, and which this essay too exemplifies.

I wonder how de Man might have written his own memoir or "confession." Shoshana Felman has argued that he did so, in effect: his silence was not a silence insofar as his writings after a certain turning point, perhaps beginning in late 1942, constituted an attempt to "wake up," to separate from the past and expose the error that went into his political misjudgment. He did not feel his mistake was simply a personal mistake: it was widespread and with implications that demanded, in order to be set right, the most sustained analysis of "cette perpétuelle erreur, qui est précisément la 'vie,'" "that perpetual blunder which 'life' is, quite precisely," to cite the quote from Proust he used as epigraph for his first collection of essays, *Blindness and Insight*.

Derrida too suspects that de Man's experience of error was worked into his mature essays, like that on Rousseau's "Excuses (Confessions)." De Man may have "impersonified" himself through Rousseau. No doubt it is heavy going to follow de Man on Derrida on Rousseau, and Derrida on de Man on Rousseau. While I find this sustained exchange and its oblique circuitry remarkable, I come away with an uncomfortable sense of glosses turning into glossolalia. The richness of such metacommentary, however, continued by Derrida after his friend's death—keeping him alive, in a way—never quite loses sight of the "referential reading moment," or what Michel Leiris calls, in his famous book on *The Autobiographer as Torero*, "the deadly horn of the bull."

Yet here my ability to judge reaches a limit. The errors in my life have not necessitated a self-silencing by way of an impersonal writing, although I have stood near that precipice. I have not had to break with a past or turned to words that could be charged with hiding the truth. There have been shocks, regrets, moments of acute self-doubt and self-blame, as well as despair about the miseries that spirit as well as flesh is heir to. Many times I feel impotent and depressed in the face of political enormities, of manmade ravages that seem to destroy any pastoral, let alone utopian hope. But I cannot say that my personal life, or the part of it for which I am directly responsible, contains a nightmare from which I am trying to awake, and that this has determined my intellectual journey. There is no incident with a fatal and malevolent result to which I have consciously contributed and that has to be dealt with by excising a previous self or creating in reaction an impersonal and devious discourse, as if fleeing from a persecution of myself by myself, from a Pascalian sense that the I is "haïssable," unredeemably shameful. Whatever my motives are in writing this memoir, they do not rise to a "justification egotisée,"[34] as Derrida called autobiography.

Not that my way of speaking about literature in relation to life is all that forthright. Browning said that Christopher Smart, in his poetry, tried to pierce "the screen / Twixt thing and word." He "lit language straight from soul." I consider that a mad and heroic endeavor beyond

84

my capacities. It is because I am devoted to keeping literary thinking alive as a meditative and humanizing mode, and not because I flee from the past, that I work, think, and witness from a secondary zone.

A memoir writer, of course, is bound to migrate into the past as if it belonged to someone else, to an intimate stranger. That past is not past, however, and hardly ever inert. It tells me it is there, still functioning, like the steady blinking of an alarm, one that suddenly sounds off without apparent cause.

De Man's legacy remains in dispute and therefore alive. It is supportive yet also deeply critical of what has come to be called the Enlightenment project. Those who have read him will pay greater attention to the irony that literary criticism progresses, if at all, by an accumulation of negative rather than dogmatic interpretations. The pattern is that each brand-new critic complains about a previous critic's misreading, yet always represents that "as a contingent, never as a constituent obstacle to literary understanding." While in science, according to Gaston Bachelard's *Philosophie du non*, such polemics lead to revisions and discoveries, in literary commentary, according to de Man, they highlight a "systematic avoidance of the problem of reading, of the interpretive or hermeneutic moment."

De Man seeks to clarify rather than resolve this instability of interpretive reading. Bachelard thinks that scientists build a "surobjet" but also

De Man's critique of the metaphysics of presence in literary criticism, literary history, and the notion of modernity. The constitutive instability of interpretive reading. Dwelling in (rather than on) the negative. His kind of mental power and the distrust it elicits. Effect of the discovery of an occluded biographical dimension on

the theorist's
authority. A final
uncertainty. that their revisions gradually subvert it. As we
might now say, the paradigm morphs into something totally different. The literary object, however, is not such a speculative construct; interpretive
error, moreover, has a dynamic weave of its own that cannot be removed from the concept of the literary and its
tropological complexities.

It is frustrating to remain in the negative with de Man.
He is a connoisseur of nothingness. The "Criticism and
Crisis" essay in *Blindness and Insight* observes of Rousseau that in him "consciousness does not result from the
absence of something, but consists of the presence of a
nothingness. Poetic language names this void with ever-
renewed understanding." The way de Man stays on message and does not dignify the void by giving it an existentialist or religious turn has the unexpected effect of telling
us more about literariness than do "substantive" theories
grounding the importance of literature in positive ethical
or directly functional considerations. Literature, then,
does not compensate an absence nor collaborate with current theories claiming for the aesthetic effect imagistic or
other types of fullness. Identifying the "presence of a
nothingness" with consciousness, and especially literary
consciousness, joins de Man to Derrida's critique of a
metaphysics of presence.

Especially persuasive is de Man's demonstration that
the category of literary modernity, its emphasis on a pre-
emptive present, and literary history (the canonical
sequence that determines the meaning and value of
authors), unsettle each other. Critics who accept that the
diachronic order of artifacts is significant yet propose at

the same time that their readings are a rupture or radically new departure seem blind to the pattern they repeat. In claiming to be modern, in enacting "the persistent temptation of literature to fulfill itself in a single moment," they cancel out their historically mediated position, the contingent status of their own words. De Man sometimes calls this a "temporal dilemma." Such contradictory assertion and erasure of our temporal situation also marks the object of analysis, the literary artifact. It is "constitutive of literary consciousness and has to be included in a definition of the specificity of literature."[35]

In views antagonistic to de Man, during his life and after it, the suspicion lurks, and sometimes rises to the surface, that he was a confidence man. Not in the vulgar sense that his intellectual gift was used for material gain but rather that, as if the reason for his deception lay deep within reason itself, a person of his mental power set out to deceive others in order to test and mock their intellectual pretensions.

This suggests something implausible. In the sphere of religion or politics there are false leaders, false prophets. But in philosophy or literature—apart from religious or ideologically motivated forgers? The stakes do not seem high enough. Exception might be made for Leo Strauss and adepts who see truth telling as so dangerous that it necessitates, in philosophically worthy writing, a division between its exoteric and esoteric levels of meaning, between initiates and outsiders. Charges that someone is a fraud or charlatan amount usually to a base and envious reaction by those who distrust a species of mental power: ironic, agnostic, riddling, skeptical.

What we continue to seek from the kind of thinking that does not renounce the search for truth yet refuses to say that truth once attained will be comforting and resolving—what we ultimately respect is the very effort involved in attempting to purge appearances, to separate reality from its illusory doubles, even if that proves to be an endless task. Were a philosopher unmasked who claimed to have pursued this endless end, were such a one really shown to be a false guru, would those nearest to him not have to say: "We knew it, but failed him, failed his own lesson, which he has now taught us by a message from the very realm of death? We failed to understand that there is no absolute way of distinguishing once and for all what is semblance from a truth free of it." Yet such a redemptive move is too easy, too much like the habit of apocalypticists who recalculate the end of the world after each prophesied doomsday has passed uneventfully.

From that perspective, what de Man's silence about his past together with his antipsychologistic stance produced was an aporia or undecidable result: precisely the fact that we cannot tell whether there was an intentional deception. This uncertainty involves his later prose: blind, or was it blind, to the possibility of being rebiographied and so, however apparently impersonal, diminishing the intellectual pressure he himself helped to impose. Did he deceive us or did he merely deceive himself? Is it in the nature of the intellect, when unconditionally followed through, to create this more than literary irony? And is our only and dubious escape from indeterminacy, its "mirror upon mirror mirrored," that, having abandoned theodicy, we enter with Rousseau an age of egodicy?

Thinking back to de Man's refusal to see he was ill that summer of 1982 at the School of Criticism and Theory, perhaps the simplest explanation is that he was in denial, or lived with the constant knowledge of being in denial.

De Man died just as his formalism—stricter than that of the New Critics—was beginning to be questioned by cultural studies, the New Historicism, and the women's movement. These restored in force what he had analyzed as dilemmas intrinsic to literary acts. Issues came to the fore again concerning the concept of identity, personal or collective, especially its relation to socioeconomic forces within the colonial and imperialistic cultures that foment wars and genocides. De Man's close reading was admired only insofar as it demystified—demonstrated the blindness of—ideological positions that denied their own mediated status, verbal traps Nietzsche called "petrified, eternalized words" that laid claim, against time, to a privileged truth.[36]

The Fateful Question of Culture. **Cultural studies and the new materialism. Aestheticide. Multiculturalism, and the economy of emotional investments. Culture receives a militant connotation. Raymond Williams's "long revolution." Wordsworth's long-range influence on English culture.**

In the wake of de Man, literature is demoted once more to the status of auxiliary proof: an illustration of social and political determinants rather than a primary contestation. My own increased concern, which led to *The Fateful Question of Culture* (1997), was twofold. The literary text was being dissolved into context or materialistic motivation, with the art in art isolated or marginalized as a superstructural "aesthetic ideology." In a later book, *Scars of the Spirit* (2002), I devoted an essay to this "aestheticide." A simplified and categoric rather than careful reintegration of the historical consciousness was eliding the open or indeterminate moment of interpretation in order to produce political messages.[37] Every gap, distancing, or reticence tended to be denounced as a repression or evasion of the sociopolitical realities.

Moreover, the liberal and cosmopolitan overtones that used to characterize the word "culture" (*The Fateful Question* traced its semantic vicissitudes) were giving way to a militant denotation. I was reminded of the kind of culture politics that had played a malignant role in the Franco-German rivalry (an intra-European "clash of civilizations") from the late nineteenth century on. But now, in an ironic twist, the very generosity animating multiculturalism became imperious, divisive, and surprisingly unrealistic in its assumption that we were endowed with unlimited resources of empathy. The more that magnanimity was insisted on, the more the question had to be raised whether the economy of emotional life makes such an ideal feasible. Are we in the grip of a demand that is utopian rather than realistic?

Often in urban renewal, when one city block has been renewed, another falls vacant. So a "sympathy paradox" is observed whereby the emotions turn, guiltily, to a neglected victim group, only to become indifferent to another victim group, or even to find a scapegoat for intolerable injustice and misery. Morality faces a bitter question. Can our limited sensibility be overcome? Can Eros be converted into a moral energy without reserve? Or, do orgiastic-saintly efforts lead to personal or even collective and sometimes suicidal emotional expenditures? Georges Bataille, Antonin Artaud, and Deleuze and Guattari should be considered in the light of these questions.

Outside France too, of course, important presences like Raymond Williams faced that broader "economic" issue, one inclusive of the emotions. Williams as cultural critic respected local "structures of feeling" that resisted the nation-state's triple whammy of centralization, rationalization, and specialization. He was aware of the trauma inflicted as commerce and industrialization transformed country and town, changing Britain rapidly from a primarily agrarian to a modern capitalistic economy. An urban type of misery arose (including a homelessness beggaring that of the countryside), and a class of intellectuals often slandered as "rootless cosmopolitans."

The attempt to avoid capitalism by switching to a totally planned economy had its own tragedy. In Stalin's Russia, Mao's China, and with even bloodier consequences in Cambodia, huge population shifts enforced a mental reorientation backed up by massive and repressive schemes of reeducation. The dislocations and migrations have not ended, so that the divorce of imaginative habits from more "organic" rhythms or customs that seem natural is still ongoing in many parts of the globe.

The Fateful Question urged critics interested in the social text not to neglect the complexity of literature, given the deadly fallout of *dirigisme*, planification, and simplistic political ideologies. Exploitative politicians as well as power-starved intellectuals tend to serve up a retrospective and nostalgic picture of rural life in order to peddle fascistic and corporatist remedies, or, going in the opposite direction, to urge an urbanization involving the resettlement/reformation of the peasantry—with cata-strophic consequences. In America, until recently, a stan-dard ploy of those running for office was to claim they or their immediate ancestors hailed from small-town or rural regions, as if such closeness to the soil guaranteed a special degree of authenticity. The vital issue that gets lost is the prevention of famine and achieving agricultural sus-tainability supported by a cultural respect for traditional practices.

If a more gradual or "Long Revolution," as Williams called it, moderated the ravages in Britain, diminishing fanaticism and extreme ideologies, would it not be *also* because of Wordsworth, followed by George Eliot and other writers who did not want the imagination alienated from the English countryside and who kept hope in a slower, harmonious rate of modernization alive? A tradi-tion was created that culminated in a social visionary like John Ruskin, haunted in the last part of the nineteenth century by symptoms of actual changes not only in the environment but fatally in nature itself. Sure that an omi-nous storm cloud hovered over England, he sensed the climate deteriorating, both spiritually and in actual physi-cal terms. Apocalyptic thoughts assailed him in the wake of England's rampant industrialization. His ideas on political economy in *Unto This Last* may have had a greater influence than Marx on the early British Labour Party.

It is no accident, likewise, that a literary critic, Walter Benjamin, articulated some of the most incisive observa-tions about the loss of "experience" in the period of mod-ern warfare and urban life, a loss compounded by mass media that pretend to put us in touch with reality but often substitute a semblance of communication, an abstract immediacy.[38] The early Soviet filmmakers, devoted to the genre of documentary, and Siegfried Kracauer in his film theory, acknowledged that weakening of a sense of the real, not excluding physical reality.

"Bliss was it in that dawn to be alive." So Wordsworth on the impact of the French Revolution. "And to be young," he continued, "was very Heaven." I take a step back to the 1970s and early 1980, when I was already in my Middle Years. Revolutions, moreover, tend to be false dawns. Still, I admit: the activity at Yale was infectious. Literary studies rocked at that time with palpable excitement. Graduate students and even undergrads flocked to Derrida's lectures, however lengthy and difficult. De Man, Hillis Miller, Harold Bloom, and Shoshana Felman, different as they were, generated a buzz that spread beyond their university but was not always well received. We committed the unpardonable academic sin of reading one another's work and commenting on it.

Promising younger scholar-critics were emerging too, and a majority of strong traditional scholars completed the cast. Yet because a new vocabulary and a more strenuous form of interpretation initially complicated rather than facilitated access to the text, and because presence seemed to dissolve into issues of representation, the ensuing theory turmoil was called antihumanistic in many quarters.

At Yale too there was unease. William Wimsatt Jr., esteemed Yale critical theorist and teacher, who loved to sit and argue at Naples, a local pizza joint, wrote an essay

Leopards at Yale.

on "Day of the Leopards," his title conflating an allusion to the Black Panthers with the famous anecdote in Kafka about leopards that break into the temple and empty the sacred chalices. This happens again and again until it becomes part of the temple ceremony. Interested in the closeness of sacred and saturnalian, I had cited that parable in an essay on "Structuralism: The Anglo-American Adventure" published in 1966; Wimsatt picked up on its relation to the atmosphere of protest in the sixties, and in particular the turmoil roused by the Black Panthers in New Haven. But he neglected my rather packed, conservative argument about art as a defense against social disintegration, a defense that challenged, at the same time, society's "Fables of Identity" (to steal a Northrop Frye phrase) while searching for a more durable myth of unity. It was my first formal engagement with myth criticism and literary anthropology as they converged on the structuralism of Lévi-Strauss.

Wimsatt's pamphletlike rejoinder, a version of which was delivered at Yale as early as 1968, started by quoting R. P. Warren and Robert Brustein as well as myself. Alarmed, he also, in this volume of which "Leopards" is the title essay, accused many of the post–New Critics of "battering the [literary] object." He might as well have said "vaporizing the object," since he complained—identifying Hillis Miller with the Geneva School—that such an approach resulted, for example, in "a fine mist of the mind of Hopkins."[39]

Others too, like William Pritchard at Amherst, wondered—even after the atmosphere of political crises had somewhat abated—what ungenteel things were being perpetrated by a "hermeneutic mafia," especially at Yale.

The world's body seemed at risk, the Real in all its phenomenal, ethical, and social impact.

A colleague from the Law School discerned a "new nihilism." It threatened, he claimed, "our social existence and the nature of public life," and, as if that were not enough, "demeans our lives." It was, he concluded, "the deepest and darkest of all nihilisms."[40]

The concern for public life, or what was happening to participatory democracy and public discourse as the university population grew even while reading competence (except of consumables) declined—that concern, I agree, was clear and justifiable. The general dumbing down, moreover, was not helped by a reliance in academic circles on coteries and their idiolects. I nevertheless defended the inventiveness of technical terms and the practice of a polysemic and micrological type of reading. I did not see (and to this day do not see) why that should exclude another style, a delivery system, as it were, that through book reviews and essays for the general (nonspecialized) reader broadens interest in the language of literature and everything implied by so remarkable an acquisition. We need more amphibians.

Part of the hostile reaction to what was happening at Yale may have been the plain old fear of losing students. The pang of losing touch, or fearing to lose it. The fear of having the young seduced by strange fire. For everything radical at that time, or what seemed to be so, attracted. I will describe one event.

In 1975 (the exact date remains vague in my mind), I invited Jacques Lacan to Yale. From my point of view it turned out to be a disastrous visit, since the host had to

Lacan's enigmatic incursion. deal with Lacan's array of idiosyncrasies and the lecture he gave was at once memorable and unpardonable. He made his grand entrance twenty minutes late, spent another ten having his assistant pin up colored diagrams of Borromean knots, then proceeded to no more than half an hour's intelligible discourse followed by nearly an hour of unintelligible elaboration. The law school auditorium, the venue for this talk on "The Symptom," was overfull: standing room only, with probably four hundred crowded in. No one gave up and left, although Lacan's talk was in French. Sitting in the front row, I heard him mutter as the applause subsided: "Only in America would they applaud so irritating a lecture." The word used for "irritating" was "emmerdant."

Scars of the spirit. The pathos critics like de Man had tried to purge soon flooded back. An apocalyptic tone, no less virulent because secular, entered the debates. Not until many years later, in *Scars of the Spirit: The Struggle Against Inauthenticity* (2002), did I fully understand the alarm and the bitterness. It was in response to a riptide of unrealism already beginning to affect both verbal and visual media and proceeding from the confluence of two converging factors: a frustrated striving for more and more realism and a technologically enhanced "overload of faked reality."[41]

Anti-intellectualism is not new to American life, but now, because of the media's increased power of simulation abetted by deceptive images, a quasi-gnostic distrust, a skepticism concerning what to believe, undermined the entire culture, including the political process. This in turn bred new fundamentalisms. An exploding proliferation of simulacra exacerbates the struggle against inauthenticity and motivates the search for literalism, for original intent, for a way to distinguish decisively fiction and reality, fakery and news, at a time when perspectivism, disinformation, interpretive spin, propaganda—especially via the media's potential for mass deception—infiltrate every aspect of daily life. The *malin génie* Descartes conjured up and then dismissed in order to assure himself of his own existence and the potential truth of his thoughts returns as the eternal trickster lurking in appearances and hinting once more at a repressed stratum of misprision and error.

This was the terror before the terror to come. Given such basic queasiness, did it matter that Romanticism had been revalued, philosophical texts and existential issues opened to linguistic analysis, and literary criticism—now difficult, boundary crossing, nongenteel—had refreshed itself?

The School of Criticism and Theory. Feminist confrontations.

The new spirit in criticism, which turned toward both Continental thought and a more intense scrutiny of the most serious game around, that of language, was not limited to Yale. Murray Krieger, with whom I had become friendly at the University of Iowa, founded the School of Criticism and Theory at UC Irvine in 1976. Its mission was to increase access to new developments in literary theory and practice. Krieger had been a pioneer supporter of the New Criticism, bringing it to the academy via courses in critical theory in the 1950s.

When he wished to give up his summer institute, I agreed to take it over and directed the program from 1981 to 1987, first at Northwestern, then at Dartmouth. The school, now at Cornell, continues strong and has just marked its thirtieth year. It has had the help of some of the most adventurous teachers in philosophy and history as well as literary and cultural studies.[42]

During my tenure as director, feminism was on the rise and demanded a "Criticism of Our Own" (Elaine Showalter). There were quite a few tumultuous meetings. Nothing was deemed to be accidental: in one of the school's plenary sessions, even the seating arrangement (in a standard auditorium, not a circle but rising front to back) was challenged as authoritarian. Everything literary and nonliterary came under scrutiny for its possible symbolic or ideological implications. A formidable intellectual energy was released, spiked by an unrestrained use of "patriarchal," "hegemonic," "phallologocentric," etc. Women's "cultural work," in Jane Tompkins's conception, also expanded the menu of criticism.

An interesting charge at one of our plenary meetings was that women were unwilling to give up their lack of power. Should they be willing to do so, it would bestow moral authority on them as well as lead to greater representation and influence. I thought there was a problem of abdication for men too, but in reverse: of how to give up portions of established authority in ways that would promote distributive justice rather than just giving up.

One problem often raised in heated discussions was the nature of the rhetoric employed. It could be angry and close to sectarian in its exclusive political focus on women's issues. Gerald Graff, for instance, complained about a new parochialism. The focus should always be on, or come back to, cultural criticism, to issues of educational policy generally. Political rhetoric, I added, was often slander in the guise of analysis. But there is no question that woman students in graduate school, aspiring to enter the profession, had met, and sometimes were still meeting, hurtful and prejudicial statements.

Affirmative action was necessary at all levels: not only in hiring, where decisions were difficult even without that pressure, but in mentoring and encouraging women to pursue university careers.

The challenge to settled pieties sometimes took a puritanical, as well as political, turn. The argument was heard, for instance, that there were no tolerable male fantasies (such as Picasso's bullish "The Artist and his Model" pictures): that the male gaze had to be tamed. A rumor circulated in one of our summers that the "Intellectual Loveboat," as I liked to call it, had not led, for once, to amorous adventures, and this was blamed (by the men) on Aristophanean feminist solidarity. Yet gender and sexual issues, as well as other confessional experiences of the participants, entered the discussions freely. Some were made uncomfortable by that, especially women scholars from outside the United States, who supported a broader cultural criticism but viewed the emphasis on male dominance as a peculiarly American distraction.

What interested everyone, men and women alike, was the issue of the, or a, feminine sensibility; presenters like Gayatri Spivak (whose 1982 lecture at the school had an almost shock-jock effect on some, by introducing the terms "clitoris" and "faking orgasm") stimulated debates on what an *écriture feminine* would look like. Was Molly's monologue in Joyce's *Ulysses* the pattern, was Derrida's concept of "plural style" the way toward it, or explicitly feminist models emerging in France? The issue of style (including critical style) was of special interest to me. The rescue work accomplished by Gilbert and Gubar brought forward a submerged corpus of women's literary work, but one (it could be argued) stylistically still part of the dominant culture.

Yet an invaluable contribution of feminist criticism was indeed its restitutive effort, even if much of the creative contribution of women to the arts seemed irretrievably lost. Might this loss afford an opportunity? As with certain Romantic entrepreneurs like Chatterton, MacPherson, or even Coleridge (in his pseudoarchaic "Ancient Mariner"), a new tradition could be created, new role models magically retrieved from the past. Those ancestors would have to be imagined—perhaps by inventing found manuscripts, perhaps by creating personae like Shakespeare's sister, perhaps by renewing genres like the ballad. Even should feminist criticism not achieve its missing past by these devices, its future might be secured by questioning a rule-bound literary purity that historically had overreacted to anxieties about disorder in the House of Literature or the fear that literary standards would drown in effluvia of innovation. A deconstruction of the exclusionary dichotomies described in Foucault's *The Order of Discourse* was overdue.

I cite a stanza from a ditty composed in the froth and fervor of that time, a country-blues sort of mock. Called "The Deconstruction Blues," it was written by Dwight

Eddins to lighten a lecture I gave in Morgan Hall of the University of Alabama:

> Had a dream last night, nearly drove me insane.
> Thought I saw Geoffrey Hartman in a giant crane.
> Said, "What you doin' with that wreckin' ball?
> He said "I'm deconstructin' old Morgan Hall."
> I said "Geoff, you can't do that." He said "Don't be Saussure!
> I got it right down here in *écriture*
> That I'm supposed to give you damn New Critics hell,
> And have your phonemes disconnected by Southern Bell."
> CHORUS
> I got them low-down, spin-around deconstruction blues,
> Call Yale every morning, find out the latest views.
> They told me "Read your Derrida, DeMan, DaBloom and all 'dem groovy books;
> Stay away from fancy women, fancy liquor, and Cleanth Brooks!"[43]

How does one gauge progress in the humanities? Something always falls away, unjustly. Literary structuralism—inspired by Saussure's semiotics, Propp's morphology of narrative, Jacobson's linguistics, and Lévi-Strauss's anthropological elaboration—had barely made its appearance in North America when it was almost elided by poststructuralism under the influence of Derrida. In continental Europe, it lasted much longer (think of Roland Barthes, whose

Interchapter: style as battleground.

career spans both structuralist and poststructuralist analysis); it is still accepted there as the scientific side of humanistic studies, or that aspect likely to persuade governmental bodies to fund literary research. But an explosion, often descriptively simplified as "theory," also challenged the communicative mode of the conversational ("familiar") essay, which had dominated literary culture in England and was the mainstay of *belles-lettres* journalism both there and in America.

The contemporary give and take of discursive styles is complex and, on the whole, or so I believe, fruitful. It is particularly interesting in the United States, with its large number of major universities. Inevitably, a coterie forms in these centers, with a presiding genius (or several such djinns): this limits intellectual vision but also allows local differentiation. While there is considerable uniformity within each corporate fellowship of teachers and students, nationally these provisional centers jostle and conflict.

Internationally, no other system of higher education is as lively. Yet given the very large number of students who enter the American university, many needing instruction in the basics of literate English, a plethora of textbooks on literary theory and criticism cut everything up into "movements," and—despite the new personalism—fail to respect the issue of critical style.

Simplified umbrella terms commodify critical movements and are seized upon by publishers as good advertising copy for profitable textbooks—even while valuable first monographs by fledgling scholars find difficulty being published. This encourages neither good history nor good writing. It is as if personal style in literary commentary were an undefinable value. No wonder critical writing is held to be uncreative or purely fashionable. A saving illusion is fostered, at the same time: that it is possible to construct a story out of the movement of these movements and so claim a redeeming if minor sociological interest.

There is, doubtless, a collective as well as individual component in significant critical writing. I am far from sure how important it is. The pressure of the collective on individual thought can be enabling, but also disabling, depending on the quality of our resistance to it. Moreover, essayistic criticism cannot become an *oeuvre* unless one is a Montaigne or Emerson, writing about many aspects of human life or pursuing a larger career in the world of art. Essayists have to create, as it were, an environment of their own.

Even minutiae matter. Writers, in whatever genre, have the experience of finding in their work not only outworn phrases but startling jumps, peculiar transitions, non sequiturs. Their style is also vulnerable to restitutive adjustments (as simple as "his or her"). In the long run, there is a winnowing of these elements according to the writer's intensity of thought and integrity of expression. Such qualities are not easily evaluated in terms of progress. They may contribute, in fact, to a deliberate reticence or avoidance of opinion. In the essay, dogma is now replaced by a methodical doubt, including (as in Derrida) a conceptual tick that pronounces decisive assertions to be at once crucial and "impossible."

Style often becomes a battleground. Those most positive or pretentious in denouncing the decadence of their time, and who invariably attack the style of critics they resent, belie their own vision by the very ferocity with which they impose it. The impression given is that they stand in fear of personal decline and need an enemy to self-invigorate. I find my judgment of both past and present too variable to see a single, necessary path to salvation, but this does not imply I do not cry out, at times, or forfeit all judgment. It does mean an awareness, which one's style reflects, of alternate paths that can or should be tried, as in a maze worth exploring for its own sake, even if not all its turnings lead to a dazzling way out.

Judaism and Judaic studies at Yale. The founding of a new field is quite unusual in the humanities, and is certainly one sign of progress. Judaic studies as a degree-granting program got its start on American campuses only in the 1970s and 80s.

In 1955, when I began to teach, even a purely cultural interest in Judaism was merely tolerated by Yale's distinctive, if quietly assumed, Christian ethos. In some quarters, there were doubts as to whether a non-Christian could really appreciate a literary tradition so strongly based on Christian faith and symbolism. Ironically, I found myself having to instruct undergraduates about the basic symbols of their faith so that they might understand such canonical authors as Spenser, Donne, and Milton.

There was no visible sign of Judaic origins anywhere, except on Yale's escutcheon. Jewishness was a private matter; Hillel a hole in the wall in a basement on the Old Campus. The number of (putative) Jewish professors in the College of Arts and Sciences did not outnumber the fingers of one hand. Paul Weiss in philosophy was a resident Diogenes, and the most affable, ubiquitous, belligerent, unbelieving Jew around. My interest in Jewish history and literature was confined to sneaking into classes a few textual nuggets from that source and meeting irregularly with a faculty group.

I left Yale in 1962 for the University of Iowa and then Cornell to take up tenured positions in comparative literature, but also because of signs that my work did not interest senior colleagues at Yale. (I have already mentioned spending the 1960 to 1961 academic year as a visitor at the University of Chicago.) Called back to Yale five years later, I learned from a colleague who had been at the university in the 1940s about the fuss made when Lionel Trilling's nomination was proposed early that decade. He also revealed that a superior committee had, in an unusual move, overturned the recommendation of Yale's English department, placing two junior colleagues with a less productive record of publication above Harold Bloom and myself in the annual contest for the Morse faculty fellowship.

I never encountered any *overt* sign of prejudicial behavior during my first appointment at Yale. Disinterest, yes, but not overt discrimination. It did strike me as peculiar, therefore, when, after receiving the tenure offer from Iowa, a distinguished elder of the department, who had rarely spoken to me, journeyed across a large room in the university library to pump my hand and congratulate me on the offer.

Gradually, the atmosphere changed. Judah Goldin, an eminent scholar of Midrash, was active at Yale by 1959;

the admission criterion of "character," code for non-Jewish, especially non–New York Jewish, became less important than intellectual promise, and this propelled the number of Jewish students well above the previous 9 to 10 percent, as Yale's entering classes were diversified in the 1960s through the policies of Kingman Brewster, his dean of admissions, Inky Clark, and the social activism of the university chaplain William Sloane Coffin. A general expansion of the university also brought more Jews into the humanities faculty.

Perhaps because it was hard to separate gentility from privacy, or because senior colleagues were in great demand elsewhere, though pride in Yale was strong, the faculty's communal spirit was weak. In the humanities, the boundary between departments was rarely crossed; both Yale College and the graduate school had none of that mix of social and intellectual activities so vital in today's campus. The admission to Yale College in 1969 of a significant and increasing number of women certainly helped the momentum of change. African American studies, too, got a wonderful start in the early 1970s with Charlie Davis, who brought in Henry Louis (Skip) Gates and Robert Stepto, among others. David Brion Davis also joined the faculty. In the later 1970s, a committee I chaired at Kingman Brewster's request, with kindred spirits that included (to the best of my recollection) David Apter, Peter Gay, Jerry Pelican, and Bart Giamatti, banded together to promote collegial exchanges within the university and transform an initiative of the National Endowment for the Humanities into the Whitney Humanities Center. During this period I also continued an autodidactic effort to read the classics of the Jewish tradition; this helped to motivate a commitment to Yale when it finally set up a program in Judaic studies.

One eventually sees what is before one's eyes: a lack, a bias, a distortion. So my interest in Judaic studies did not come primarily from the frustrated sense of community mentioned above. Rather, a growing impatience to have the university curriculum enriched was moved by a strong sense of what was missing. Where was the harvest of German Jewish scholarship before it was brutally cut off; where was the fatally wounded Yiddish culture of Poland and Eastern Europe? Instruction was offered in conversational Hebrew, yet the two-millennia-plus tradition of Jewish social and cultural history, as well as a biblical commentary spanning many countries, was left to one senior faculty member (or two junior ones) added to non-Judaic-studies-trained scholars of the Scriptures and the intertestamental period. I pointed out, testily, that, in contrast, there were five tenured appointments in pagan studies, as I called it, a.k.a. the classics.[44]

Chance intervened in the person of Bart Giamatti, Yale's new president, who came to a similar conclusion about that imbalance. He asked me to head a fundraising drive to expand teaching resources in Judaic studies. Together with William Hallo (curator of the Babylonian collection as well as biblical scholar and translator of Franz Rosenzweig's *Star of Redemption*), I also coordinated policy for the new major. Between 1981 and 1987, most of my time was spent on these tasks. I did not consider Judaic studies as an identity-affirming program but as the recovery of a historical source whose neglect was impoverishing secular education as well as leaving dangerous stereotypes intact.[45] Eventually, too, through the persistence of James Ponet, director of Hillel at Yale, the Slifka Center was built in 1995 to replace makeshift lodgings and create a gathering place for many campus-wide cultural as well as religious Jewish activities.

Founding of Yale's video archive for Holocaust testimonies. It was also around 1980, as I passed my fiftieth year, that the opportunity came to do something active about the memory of the Holocaust. A disturbing and extra-academic route of inquiry opened up.

My wife, Renée, is a child survivor of the Holocaust. At the age of ten, she and her deaf younger sister Hertha were deported from Bratislava to the Bergen-Belsen concentration camp. The sisters had been sent to hide in farms known to the deaf community. But when their parents were deported to Auschwitz in 1944 and payments to the people sheltering the children stopped, Renée and Hertha returned to their home town, now emptied of Jews except for a remnant in hiding. After a time, they had to give themselves up to the local police. The girls barely survived their year in the camp.

Renée warned me against getting involved; she feared it would become an obsession. But I joined her in supporting a grassroots New Haven group started by a plucky television interviewer, Laurel Vlock, and a Yale psychiatrist, Dori Laub (himself a child survivor). They had begun videotaping Holocaust witnesses, including Renée. The question faced by the group was how to expand their effort to reach beyond New Haven.

I was struck by the project's relevance for education in an audiovisual age. Yale might archive and curate it properly, catalogue it for intellectual access, and allow it to expand nationally and internationally. Accepted by the university in 1981, the Fortunoff Video Archive for Holocaust Testimonies (named by Alan Fortunoff, a major benefactor, in memory of his parents) set the standard for careful taping, brought the video recording of witnesses to Europe and Israel, and helped to overcome a prejudice against oral history that met us at the outset. Later, viewing the official activity in France as it recorded the memories of World War II veterans for the 2005 anniversary, especially of deported and imprisoned *résistants*, it was hard to imagine the penury of oral documentation efforts twenty-five years earlier.

I thought of myself only in terms of organizer and fundraiser. Yet the complex presuppositions of such an archive, one that combined oral documentation and the medium of television, gradually overtook the necessity of having to "sell" the undertaking to foundations and individual donors. Developing the archive also meant visiting many countries to establish affiliates that recorded culture-specific perceptions and especially the survivors' postwar struggles for social reintegration. These stories of resettlement and return to life are as moving and essential as the passion narratives brought from the camps and hiding places.

As Renée had foreseen, most of my recent work has been touched by what I learned from collecting Holocaust testimonies. It is influenced no less, however, by the issue of how we face catastrophe in an era of "souffrance à distance" (suffering conveyed and induced by distant events), as the French sociologist Luc Boltanski has named it. Through the media, we have become involuntary spectators and impotent bystanders of widespread political terror and the misery it leaves behind.

Memory, whether it is the reflection of scenes directly experienced or those disseminated by the media, is more than a mimetic and retentive faculty. It is a field of strife, since the perpetrators or their sympathizers continue cultivating falsifications responsible for the outbreak. The war against memory often flares up. Holocaust denial is only one, if extreme, example. A counteraction through historical research, testimony projects, Truth Commissions, and organizations like *Nunca Mas* has a chance of overcoming a helpless grief. As I write this, the "Artemis Project" has been launched at Yale to safeguard and provide access to records coming out of the many Truth Commissions. These records are often endangered by continuing political conflict or lack of money and preservation expertise.

Commemorative activities usually involve various communities. Among them are the survivor generation with the courage to bear witness, the successor generation that encourages testimony and becomes a witness to the witness, and witnesses by adoption—men and women of conscience whose families were not directly affected but who accept their obligation to learn how a culture decimated by genocide remembers and transplants itself.

In the past it was the spread of empire, *translatio imperii*, or the ravages of internecine civil war, that might lead to an unexpected *translatio studii*: the reconstitution in a foreign land of the customs and culture of a persecuted people. Virgil's Aeneas is an émigré, a refugee culture bearer and the heroic expression of something that need not be militant, in the sense of founding a new imperialistic order and starting the cycle of conquest and destruction all over again. The contemporary Cambodian refugee saves a portion of her cultural memory by gardening or by participating in a new dance; a Peruvian theater collective performs an *Antigone*; in Sierra Leone, a graduate student works toward the restoration of hope with PowerPoint presentations of indigenously created memorial objects. Museums, testimonies, artworks, cenotaphic sculptures, photographic assemblages, and a seminal revival of endangered languages such as Yiddish provide templates for the persistence of the collective memory in an era of genocides.

I am often asked about my turn from Wordsworth, the Romantic poets, and reflections on the function and style of literary criticism to a focus on catastrophic trauma, the Holocaust, and the collective memory. There is no mystery:

Trauma, literature, and issues of representation.

the study of literature, like literature itself, does not shy from the painful task of considering the inhumanities of this world. Human-rights legislation is essential but cannot by itself deter xenophobia from turning into deadly hatred. Because of the excess characterizing genocide— which also affects explanation, so that the very attempt to explain, to figure out the "why" rather than the instrumental "how," has been called obscene—we tend to fall into an apologetic stutter about the ineffectiveness of culture and especially the humanities in the attempt to assure civic and human rights.

But the "obscene" is that which must be known yet may not be shown or shown only indirectly, off the scene, and this is a judgment artists continually make and critics must scrutinize. It is at the heart of all attempts to face what happened in the Holocaust and the difficulty of pursuing normal life in its aftermath. It is equally relevant to post-traumatic survival, personal or public, in the wake of other genocides.

"To explain suffering," Simone Weil wrote, "is to console it, therefore it must not be explained." To show extreme or unrelieved suffering should also be out of the question, yet there may be a necessity to show it, even if that tends to stylize suffering, as Adorno surmised, blunting shock by the very fact of routine exposure.

The heightened attention to issues of representation is precipitated, in good part, by the advent of new, supervisual media. Their mimetic power raises, however, moral rather than technical questions linked to the constant need to make decisions about what should be transmitted and with what degree of graphic virtuosity. Nor is the disaster of each genocide a finite one: Liberation did not free the Holocaust victim from a haunting return of memories.

Growing up in a family directly touched by the Shoah has been the impetus for many a tragic or tragicomic story about intergenerational trauma. Moreover, in countries like Rwanda, scarred by genocide, perpetrator and victim may have no option but to live again side by side as neighbors. And, as no war has proved to be a war to end all wars, so no genocide, we realize today, even as horrendous and total as the Shoah, has ended the outbreak of new genocides.

The field of Holocaust and Genocide studies, like the study of literature, requires not only an increased capacity for empathy, a sensitivity to the plight of others, but also

a route leading from study, theory, and contemplation to ideas on preventive and remedial

Study and action.

action. Answering this challenge promotes an analysis of
the concept of action itself. This may sound like another
diversion from action into thought. But action cannot be
divorced from agents, who remain thinking and self-justifying beings; one of the real issues, therefore, is when to
become a partisan, or plan a collective intervention that
may mean giving up a measure of personal autonomy, a
partial sacrifice of the intellect.

Another equally important issue is to understand the
testamentary role of memory and tradition. Few have
written more eloquently and precisely about that than
Hannah Arendt in prefatory reflections to *Between Past
and Future*, reflections stimulated by comments the
French poet René Char published immediately following
World War II. The tragedy *after* Liberation, Arendt
writes, began because of the totality of the collapse as well
as confusion in an atmosphere when "there was no mind
to inherit and to question, to think about and to remember." There must be, she continues, a "testament" in
Char's sense, "a thinking completion after the act." Without this "articulation accomplished by remembrance,
there simply was no story to be told."

A reminiscence. I had been invited to give a talk at Tel-
Aviv University. Free later that evening, and by myself, I
find the nearest café and sit there over my *hafuch* reading
at leisure. I notice a very elderly woman near my table
observing me. Eventually she addresses me in English:
"You like books? My father owned a bookstore in the
Old Country." She can't be picking me up, I think incon-
gruously. We start a conversation. She tells me, in a somewhat disheveled way, about the persecution and the

escape of some family members. Then she adds: "I've recorded my story. It's at Yale, in their video archive."

This is a coincidence one tolerates only in fiction. Near the end of her life, she is eager to confide, invites me to her place. I cannot refuse. It is more disheveled than her conversation. She is occasionally visited by a daughter; otherwise she does not seem to have close human contacts. She cannot find the pictures she wants to show me. Back at the Fortunoff Archive, I learn that they know her well, that she has continued being in touch. Her story is safe. A testament of sorts. A kind of completion.

Consistency in change. Dreamwork. The longest shadow. A dear friend has suggested that the change of focus in my work was an attempt to repair a discontinuity in my life.[46] I cannot deny it. Yet change has its own consistency. So the apparent discontinuities found in difficult texts or in the illogic of dreams have always challenged me to value them. Some fundamental theme or emotion is rescued and brought into the light of public scrutiny, also perhaps by this memoir.

As a child in England, I invented a ritual that already indicated the need to overcome damage from a traumatic separation by a counterseparation. Suiting action to words, I would say to myself, regularly and compulsively: I will take three steps, one, two, three, and—everything is new and happy. Because, later, the moment of finding my mother was also that of losing her again—the years of separation and having become a young adult made it difficult to identify with the stranger meeting me at the dock in 1945—that game of renewal deepened immeasurably.

A dream from my late thirties plays back my hopes—partly as wish-fulfillment images and partly as a jumble unable to cohere and integrate what I had learned of my German and religious heritage. I dreamt *my grandfather has written a memoir, published by Oxford* [that may allude to my leaving England for America instead of entering that university], *a memoir about his stay in Zürich, 1929–36. Apparently my mother and I were with him during that period.* [Here all the right archaic feelings surface: *temps retrouvé*, ancestry, family cohesion, the fake—or scholastic—certainty that comes with the punctilio of dates.] *I find myself at a Turkey dinner, then at a synagogue, where the German literary critic Friedrich Schlegel is to speak. I meet him and he remembers my grandfather ("long beard, down to here, very pious"). I come late to the synagogue and can't find the place the service has reached in the prayer book. The service is in Hebrew, and my prayer book has only English.*

The dream occurred some time after Thanksgiving and before "Christmas-Chanukah." The note recording it indicates that I had been thinking about syncretism and its axiom ("La Nature aime les entrecroisements"), reading Schlegel and other Romantic cultivators of the aphoristic fragment, and trying—once again—to sum myself up toward the future while regretting my feeble understanding of Hebrew and of Jewish ritual. The note mentions that I was strangely grateful to the dream despite its confusion. In its inchoate way it must have corroborated fugitive thoughts, giving them a memorable if quirky shape. Now, I surmised, I could no longer ignore my wish to retrieve the past—even though no real solution to how that would come about was in sight.

How could I, in any case, "integrate" the destruction I barely escaped? The shadow of the Holocaust often waylays me like the sudden darkness of a storm in the middle of a sunny day. A further dream, during the very writing of this memoir, took up the shadow metaphor as if to confirm its reality. *I am walking along a path bathed in sunlight, resembling a promenade high in the Judean hills. Below me I glimpse a beautiful landscape, a city in the valley encompassed by sheltering trees. But the heavens above that prospect suddenly grow dramatically dark.* [Later I identify the day's residue: I had looked at a reproduction of a famous El Greco painting of a scene from the life of Christ that was also, because of the elongated bodies, an ascension, and which is set against a view of Toledo bathed in a strange shadow-light.] *I am impelled to go down from the high ground to that valley and its city. But wishing to get a view that is more complete, as well as find a safe descent, I begin walking close to the edge of a sandy ridge, slip, and begin falling. I try desperately to hold on, to slow my descent, hoping to reach uninjured the radiant yet darkly enskied city, using one foot to shovel the sand against me in order to break the fall. Nothing can stop my fall, and in a near-panic I wake.*

"Speaks true, who speaks shadow" (Paul Celan). *The Longest Shadow*, essays written mainly in my sixties, traces various attempts, including my own, to engage with the aftermath of loss, with taking it into consciousness. Something, to be sure, gradually flourishes again. Yet in every generation a new threat to the Jewish people occurs, aiming at its cultural or even physical destruction, and now with scientific efficiency.

It hurts to see guards in Europe at practically every synagogue and Jewish community center. In Amsterdam, I visit Rabbi Soetendorp, who has given his testimony to the Yale archive. During the Shoah, Soetendorp escaped death as an infant when he was smuggled out of the city wrapped in a blanket. I notice how, in his synagogue, he remembers each congregant as if numbering them, or as if they were already in the space of memory, inhabiting a storylike past, having been as well as being. Most of them are survivors.

A visit to Worms, a German city associated with Rashi, one of the great medieval Bible commentators, leaves me even more uncertain about the future of the Jewish community in Europe. I support fully its casting new roots in Germany, as elsewhere. But when I hear the curator of the famous Jewish cemetery in Worms, "Der Heilige Sand," tell how it had escaped desecration, a strange and unexpected sadness comes over me. The story goes that when Himmler visited the cemetery in 1936 he pronounced it to be "etwas sonderbares" (something out of the ordinary), a comment then repeated as authoritative to ward off anyone attempting to vandalize the graveyard. Hearing this, I suddenly envision what is before me—the graveyard, the restored synagogue, its ritual bath, Rashi's study—preserved indeed, but in effect part of Hitler's infamous "Museum of a Vanished Race." It is as if everything Jewish in Germany had become a museum. The synagogue in Worms was being used only here and there for a bar mitzvah, and the curator treated every Jewish relic, great or small, as rare and instructive.

During my visits to Israel I always try to connect with one of my favorite novelists, Aharon Appelfeld. We generally meet at Beit Tycho, a cafe in Jerusalem named after the famous painter Anna Tycho. That is where he often sits and writes. One Friday, just before Shabbat, he urges me to take a walk through nearby Mea Sharim, the Orthodox quarter. Aharon suddenly turns tourist guide. As if I were a naïve visitor he forestalls my thoughts, corrects my preconceptions. "To understand Jewishness," he says, "you must come here. You see that middle-aged woman carrying home heavy bags for Shabbat? I tell you she is not oppressed but privileged." I note the children, some looking rather pale and even stunted. "Look how healthy they are. What red cheeks." He urges me to come back later, at night, to streets that at this moment are nearly empty because of the imminence of the Sabbath. The streets, he prognosticates, will be "all black, thousands."

There is Yom Hashoah, Holocaust Commemoration Day, and there is, close by, Yom Hatevah, Earth Day. We have to memorialize even the earth. We celebrate earth with song and festivity, that it is still alive and capable of giving joy despite everything: polluted, violated, a palimpsest of cemeteries, grave upon grave, corpse upon rotted corpse. Even on Earth Day, even on this beautiful spring morning, must I recall the fields of Auschwitz, Treblinka, Dachau? They are at peace now; the blood does not of itself cry from the ground. But history has become memory, and memory fights with an obligatory heaviness.

"We cannot not know the extent of political torment," Terrence des Pres has written. He adds that because of "the spectacle of man-created suffering," "a new shape of suffering invades the mind." In the early 1980s, Terrence spent a year at Yale, and we became good friends. I interviewed him for the Yale archive in his role as a witness to the witness. I had read his book *The Survivor*, a compassionate classic by a tormented man, non-Jewish, who did not evade what happened. The evil was absolute in his eyes and had to be faced by all. Others were maddened by righteous rage; Terrence knew that the problem was hatred itself, fueled by political machination. "Great hatred, little room," Yeats wrote as he saw Ireland consumed.

I turn again to the life of learning as it faces trauma and the Holocaust. Why should there be a discontinuity between the study of the arts and the urgent contemplation of extreme or traumatizing events? Even if literature itself is more reaction than action, it keeps what is crucial in mind and has the ability to touch the conscience of collectives as well as individuals.

Beginnings of an autobiography. Limits of mimesis. The Philomela project.

Beyond the matter of dreams, a quasi-autobiographical essay, "The Interpreter: A Self-Analysis" (in *The Fate of Reading*), began to breach my inner reserve. While that essay did not touch on the Holocaust, it was written in a state of excitement, as if its stylized confessions were transgressive. Like several other essays at that time (on the mystery story and on Christopher Smart), it dealt with representation-compulsion. The question that concerned me was: isn't reality enough, and too much? What motivates mimesis and the need to re-present? Is it a wish to master mentally what happened or to counter the tendency to distort or forget? Even should these motives play a role, does a graphic type of realism have to be *the* advanced mode of representation? Was classical mimesis, which maintained a certain reticence or decorum, and even cultivated the symbolic form of Pastoral because it viewed greater through lesser things—was this sort of stylization escapist, evasive, outmoded? It cannot be so, given not only the emphasis on decorum throughout the history of poetry but also the effect of well-known contemporary poems like Dan Pagis's "Testimony" and Geoffrey Hill's "September Song." The problem, as I have mentioned, is that the "obscene," if it becomes a norm of realism, threatens to habituate the consumer, or else, rendered routine, incites an escalation of special effects.

Not only academics had difficulty finding an approach to the memory of the Holocaust. Many survivors too shielded themselves from publicity well into the 1980s. They did not wish to be identified with extreme suffering. Perhaps because they feared the stigma of it, or, more likely, because what mattered to them was the life they had remade, were still remaking. If my turn to Holocaust studies did not strike me as a radical change, it was because literature and the finding or restoring of voice—the "Philomela project"—went together. In this endeavor Renée, herself a poet, has been a wonderful helpmeet. Building an archive to create conditions in which silenced voices would be heard differs from what we do in literary studies only by adding a careful application of information technology and encouraging a communiversity.

My focus on Wordsworth, which has not weakened, also confirms a broadly based interest in trauma and psychology. The poet was an eyewitness to the French Revolution from the summer of 1790 through late 1792, and he eventually experienced the deterioration of his generation's hope in the Revolution. His deception was doubly deep: not, in fact, coming

Continued relevance of Wordsworth.

primarily from the bloody, self-cannibalizing course of the revolution itself but from England's declaration of war against France, which he interpreted as the betrayal of an ideal of liberty basic to Britain's own political philosophy. One might compare his shock, followed by a disorientation powerfully described in *The Prelude*, to the disillusionment after Russia's intervention repressing the Hungarian revolt of 1956. Wordsworth's adult trauma had been preceded, however, by radical moments of fear during what he described as the heroic age of childhood. His central autobiographical issue became, therefore: how did my early nature experiences help to heal a later "internal [i.e., psychic] injury" triggered by a political event?

Because he refused to dismiss the formative impact and continuing relevance of his early nonsocialized experiences, Wordsworth's introspective poetry is always anxiously examining whether rural nature's hold on the imagination is failing. Not the death or recession of the gods concerns him, but a weakening of the rural world's influence (even of what Marx was to call "the idiocy of the village") and its consequences for the vulnerable process of individuation and socialization.

The poet's anxiety about this philanthropic ideal ("Love of Nature leading to Love of Man," to cite his heading for Book 8 of *The Prelude*) is sometimes replaced by a complacency that is hard to take. As for the possibility of avoiding or curing "internal injury," Kafka's "The

Burrow" is a powerful reminder of the suicidal character of a compulsion to attain a fortresslike invulnerability. Yet Wordsworth's claim that the Nature in the "work of mighty poets" could restore human imaginative power should not be neglected. What harnesses trauma's destructive potential, turning it toward self-development? The concept of an ecology that includes art's remedial effect continues to be relevant.

Psychoaesthetics, sound-reasoning, and the critical (un)conscious. My sporadic attempts to bring aesthetic education together with psychoanalysis led to the term "psychoaesthetics." In the 1970s, I wrote on psychoaesthetics and was the founding co-ordinator of a group at Yale that still meets regularly to discuss "Psychoanalysis in the Humanities." An essay in *Criticism in the Wilderness* charged we had neglected what Kenneth Burke called a "thinking of the body." It argued that critics, without falling into personalism, should know themselves better and analyze their relation to their calling. What does the *critic* want? Too many in our profession desire "a successful bypass of the animal, infantile, or social basis" of their needs and are willing to become functionaries, to "give up that which makes us interesting in psychological terms for an assured and stable level of functioning."[47] No wonder Freud held my attention.

I cannot figure out how much I owe to Freud, and occasionally to Lacan. My feeling is that I owe more to the "sound reasoning" (Christopher Smart's phrase) of the poets. Smart points to a reasoning based on the sound-value of words, something that would be deemed unsound by nonpoetic thinkers. Writers themselves are always struggling to avoid abandoning poetry to metaphysics or transcendental insights that exceed language as an expressive medium. So Mallarmé, working with the "hazards" of language, presents only a choice of fatalities: whatever blank-page anguish and sterility face writers who try to plumb "the mystery in letters," an equally unproductive mysticism awaits scientific purists aspiring beyond language to a univocal sign system.

The surreptitious role of the sound of words came home to me once more when invited by a psychoanalytic institute to a symposium on "The Critical (Un)Conscious." I happened to be thinking at that moment about Holocaust novels by writers born during World War II or shortly afterward. Patrick Modiano's *Dora Bruder* was one of these novels, if it can be called a novel. (Perhaps Truman Capote's term, nonfiction novel, is appropriate.) I suddenly glimpsed a peculiar affinity between Modiano and Proust on the subject of memory, an affinity that reached me via the odd pathway of a verbal accident.

Modiano as narrator and amateur historian-detective embarks on solving the case of a missing girl whose parents had taken out a "petite annonce" in a Paris paper. He says he chanced to see this personal ad some forty-seven years after it appeared in the *Paris-Soir* on the last day of 1941. What he then scrupulously reconstructs is the actual story of Dora, an adolescent runaway eventually picked up during the Paris roundups of Jews and deported to Auschwitz at the same time as her father in September 1942.

Given the French literary context, it is difficult not to think of the ad as having a haunting effect on Modiano similar to that of the "madeleine" on Proust. Yet the only connection between Dora and Modiano, in terms of their personal life, was the Paris neighborhood in which she lived, which the novelist knew well, and whose changes since the time of his youth he regrets.

The minimalism of the memory trigger in each case struck me only as forcefully as the phonetic similarity between "madeleine," "Madelaine," and "mädlein" (young girl). This associational string surprised me and seemed totally arbitrary, an absurd sonic accident. But it was certainly symptomatic of an unconscious process occurring while I was thinking about Modiano's narrative.

Moreover, though arbitrary, the punning connection was not totally unmotivated. For Modiano's storyline is not without incidents characterized by what the surrealists named a "hasard objectif." This hazard played out in my mind at the level of a similarity of sound rather than the sort of coincidence that helps to invest Modiano's book with the strangeness of a novel and turns it toward the borderline genre of autofiction. In tracing Dora's "fugue," for example, her flight from a home for girls, the author is not only reminded of his own adolescence but fantasizes about a story his father told him. In February 1942, his father crossed the path of an *inconnue*, a girl in a police van at a time when he had been arrested. Could the girl have been Dora?

Whatever unconscious process created my own interlingual cue, it made me aware not only of a similarity between Proust and Modiano but also of a significant contrast. In *Dora Bruder* a very different recovered time is depicted from that in Proust's novel. Dora-time, as I will call it, is truly *temps perdu* and unrecoverable. Or rather, this time has a double and contrasting dimension.

On the one hand, Modiano regards the Holocaust as part of his own prehistory. It is a fatal inheritance overshadowing 1945, the year he was born. He views himself quite literally a child of the Holocaust, drawn to the memory-aura of a Parisian district that feels as familiar as a *déjà vu* and which he evokes by a detailed, *nouveau roman* use of urban topography. "Les perspectives se brouillent pour moi," he says at one point, yet he holds fast to reality by means of realia, by what will strike readers as an over-specification of dates and place names, to my mind sadly like the impersonal data of bureaucratic or police files. Unrecoverable, on the other hand, and beyond that array of facts is Dora's life itself, as that of so many deported and murdered Jewish children. (Dora Bruder is listed in Serge Klarsfeld's *Mémorial* of deported Jewish children who never returned.) Like his father, Modiano crosses the path of an *inconnue*, but the son, tracking her absence, takes what responsibility he can for France's collective oblivion by penetrating and recording it.

Modiano's *recherche* does disclose, then, in the wake of Proust and as an effect of the voluntary rather than involuntary memory, an open secret. It reveals the dominant character of a time that remained partially occulted into the 1980s: the collaboration of the gendarmerie and most of the legal establishment, in Paris as in Vichy, with the Nazi regime, and this makes us fully aware of the death-bringing corruption of the French administrative and social system, a corruption without the redemptive features of Swann's society in Proust.

I cannot claim that "madeleine" "Madelaine" "Mädlein" was necessary for my understanding of the Proust-Modiano connection. Still less, that the creative unconscious actually functioned that way in Modiano. But I remain intrigued by how such verbal condensations express, as Freud showed in his analysis of dream imagery, and then of jokes and witticisms, a repressed thought, and here even the repressed memory of an era. It is unlikely that I would have arrived at this reflection without an intellectual milieu in which a poetic tradition's sound-reasoning, as well as Freud, played a major role.

Memory scars and passion narratives. Freud is astonishing: his disciplined wild side, the daring of his interpretations, hermeneutic intervention and recognition of the essential role of transference as part of any therapy, bringing dreams and unexplained physiologic symptoms into the covenant of significance, and above all, the creation of a humane treatment for those needing medical attention of a psychological kind and who had been neglected or even abused. The analytic and prophetic acumen of *Civilization and Its Discontents*, moreover, has not been surpassed. The global scope of murderous events submits the premise of civilization's progress to a devastating reality test. Can we discern any perfectibility except that of the medical and physical sciences, together with their demonic shadow: the technological enhancement of deadly weapons? "So near grows Death to Life," Milton remarks of the proximity in Paradise of the forbidden tree of knowledge to the tree of life.

Today, the surge in trauma narratives suggests that the legacy of humiliation, shame, anger, and powerlessness left by massive collective crimes or disasters must still find a creative rather than destructive outlet. It is not a good sign that a recent film of over two hours, depicting an endlessly battered male body, has drawn millions of spectators; and that an abused female body, as well as psyche, seems to be the centerpiece of many psychoanalytically oriented avant-garde theories.

I do not believe, however, that we are paying too much attention to the victims. In this one respect I totally disagree with Nietzsche's attack on compassion ("Mitleids-Moral") in his *Genealogy of Morals*. Effective or not, the meditation on suffering has its place. Passion narratives multiply and are not confined to religion. They surface as personal memoirs or as testimony about violence in a genocidal age. Maurice Blanchot's "disaster writing" is such a passion narrative, although almost devoid of confessional content. It is the patient brooding of a moralist who avoids activist clichés and pursues the negative path of an atheology rather than an explicit, positive faith or the lure of happiness. This may limit the appeal of his thought, especially with Anglo-American audiences. But it injects a realism based on the powerlessness of the "parole désarmée"[48] amid the consumable rhetoric of spectacular reality shows.

One of the last things written by Walter Benjamin contains a portrayal of the Angel of History: a figure driven forward both by his backward stare at catastrophe, which impels him to flee, and by a wind from Paradise caught in the sail of his wings. Benjamin suggests that utopian hope is part of the problem. Hope should be drawn from the past, from the "weak messianic power" of the anonymous and persecuted, rather than from futuristic promises of a millennial Eden to which populations are sacrificed.

Theories of progress can no longer be based on Hegel's thesis that "the wounds of the spirit leave no scars." A memory scar inevitably remains. Can it lead to the pursuit of justice rather than outbreaks of politicized resentment and revenge? The history each of us carries within, and the trajectory it makes us envision, should not stifle lament by turning away from harrowing testimonial narratives and the beleaguered personal memory.

Religion today. By the inverted logic of growing old, a second coming of age precedes a second childhood. I have entered that stage. A plainer style has emerged, opinions firmer or less qualified, and an outlook, unfortunately confirmed by a surfeit of 24/7 news, that not only politics and fraud are intertwined but that individual lives are, or are felt to be, deeply fraudulent. The more this feeling takes over, the more I see why a dogmatic religiosity revives in so many. It at once aggravates and provides relief for those convinced of their own hollowness or that of the human species as a whole. Like the singer Lil' Kim before going off to prison, they proclaim they have discovered a personal relationship with God as a source of redemption, of amazing grace.

The need to converse with God, that silent partner, through interior speech can be profound. This I-Thou monologue or imploration is also achieved through set forms of community prayer and their ritual repetition. But its main appeal comes from an inward and personal quality. The popularity of the Hebrew Book of Psalms and its easy adoption for Christian worship shows this. Prayer creates, like poetry, like music, and the contemplation of works of art generally, a concentrated space for inwardness. Going into the self by that path does not mean, however, separation from the community. Indeed, it often enables a going out: the individual embodying, as it were, a voice that aims to be at once polyphonic and unanimous, that rises as a choral, even an ecstatic battering at the invisible door of an invisible heart.

Yet too often there has been a willingness at the collective level to commit or condone inhumane acts in the name of religion, and so to further a particular militancy. Such transcendental violence tends to be self-justifying; it is an unfortunate aspect of the struggle against inauthenticity that reveals the scars described in *Scars of the Spirit*.

The refuge of religiosity is also corrupting in more banal ways. As I write this I come across an article about a young, depressed millionaire who found Jesus and then founded stores in Southern California malls called C28 (alluding to Colossians 2:8: "See to it that no one takes you captive through hollow and deceptive philosophy which depends on human tradition and the basic principles of this world rather than on Christ"). Innocent enough, it seems. Attractive, in fact, or so it is claimed, to a younger crowd ("Let the young children come to Me"?), his "Not of This World Merchandise" is said to be just the latest way of intertwining spiritual and market culture. Now going shopping can help you find God.[49]

At this juncture, then, and reading about such "constructive hypocrisy" (as it is called in some quarters), preacherly indignation on my part might actually be liberating. If only I were persuaded that polemics, their vigor or viciousness, would make a difference, I might find a Viagra equivalent in me to infuse my comments with something above and beyond the risk of playing to those who think the literary humanities have become nearly as corrupt and flamboyant in their exhibitionism as our decidedly unamusing corporate culture. Art can never be its own excuse, yet the energy spent in becoming a splenetic ideologue, at one and the same time merchandizing religion and branding oneself, seems merely appropriate to the American version of the "societé du spectacle," of theatricality leading to financial profit in all sectors of society, not just TV evangelism.

There is also the incredible success of the modern music industry, marketing gritty ballads composed and performed by those who turn sorrow into song, frontally exposing their life in their lyrics. They put on public display melodic spurts of a continuous passion play that competes, and easily merges with, the religious sensibility.

My own spleen may be showing here. Yet I do not believe we can return to the fabled era of Browning's Grammarian or a shabbily genteel Mr. Chips. The wicked wit detonated without shutter lag by Terry Eagleton feeds off an English society still riven by "braying" class-conscious accents and attitudes; in contemporary America, the cant is less classifiable, the eccentricities more banal, the target harder to hit. When there is a forthright and frightening attack on the pieties of U.S. politics, as in Harold Pinter's Nobel acceptance speech, it barely makes the news. Nonetheless, there is often as much lively and intelligent prose by political columnists and art reviewers on a good (not every) Sunday in the *New York Times* or the *New Yorker* as in an average week of scholarly writing.

Yet the academic writer can enhance poem, novel, film, artifact, without totally subordinating them to present-day concerns or in other ways overgoing them: something of the text, in the text, should remain strengthened, brought back into the cultural memory, even when criticized or vehemently controverted. Many today are struggling to express, as if returning to the great philosophers, the affirmative character of critique. What is unexamined is not lived.

I cannot ignore the worry that comes to me at almost every academic conference. The very power of intellect exhibited there, as colleagues

Academy and community.

go about the task of close reading, makes them, at the same time, desperate to extract, like preachers, relevant political and social messages. This tells me two things. It will not do to keep the religious imagination, deposited in texts, rituals, and modes of commentary, out of the liberal arts classroom, and confine it to divinity schools, seminaries, and religious studies departments. That's too much, in effect, like putting it in quarantine like a computer virus. It also tells me that the communitarian instinct does not die off as we pursue the teaching profession in the secular university. While advocacy should not replace analysis in the classroom, the provisional study groups we preside over, for a few months or sporadically during the four and more years of a university education, can achieve a great deal of cultural literacy, shared knowledge, and critical insight. Yet in postgraduate life this is still too rarely backed up by truly collaborative learning arrangements.

I continue to hope that quality of belief matters, and not only the specific dogma or theology involved. Faith can turn intolerant and become dangerous to civil society. The jihadists are not the only ones who, as the expression goes, hijack religion. Religious belief, therefore, should not be accorded the false respect of being shielded from debate, or restricting that exclusively to the issue of religion's influence on politics and social mores. Judaism and Christianity have fostered formidable intellects and imaginative structures. Religious wars, unfortunately, whether or not their actual cause was religious, having baptized belief with the blood of persecution, make it difficult to allow symbols, prayers, and the shared interpretation of texts to form and sustain interfaith friendships. The negative associations from the history of religious coercion prove too strong. By default, universities become seminaries for the idea, always still to be realized, of a beloved community, one that can be self-critical, marked by a continuous examination of its collective memory.

A short, generational history of reading. Toward the end of this sketch I want to give an impression of how, over the span of half a century, the practice of the ordinary and remarkable activity called reading has developed in myself, and perhaps my generation.

Yet before assuming the right to speak collectively, I must acknowledge a personal foible. For me the initial effect of words is considerably less seductive than that of music and rhythm, which have an immediate impact, at once physical and ethereal. A few bars of great music, the beginning, say, of a Beethoven string quartet or piano concerto or the soft thunder crescendos of a Brahms symphony, carry me away. I then regret the fact that I cannot pursue, after that sudden ecstatic entrapment, the complex nuances of music's changing heartbeat. Sometimes I also wish I could write at the same time with both hands, in two interactive registers, like a pianist. But I do go with the beat by a physical mimicry, discreetly nodding and swaying, like others around me. The bodily shorthand is a silent confession that I am unable to join by a silent "reading" what is going on, and hope that it is absorbed anyway, hoarded inside, a warm lining against an encroaching, permanent winter. The word-experience nearest to that musical effect is listening to a great lecturer: to Elie Wiesel, for example, who moves me, as he does the rest of his audience, by timbre and tone of voice as well as an extraordinary moral passion, giving himself totally to the task of representing not only his fellow survivors but all such victims in their grief and yearning.

Like many older people, I read slowly. Not just because I am growing old. For me it has always been so. Slow reading was a youthful and intellectual necessity that became an art. Among many in my age group likewise. We (here I assume the dubious right to speak for a plural subject) did not read to get at an idea, to extract a dominant thought, even an ideal, such as social justice. What did we read for, then; why did we read? This, even in retrospect, is a difficult question to answer.

Every youngster is in a hurry, but we knew we had a ways to go. When it came to detective novels and highly plotted, suspenseful fiction, I am sure we read as excitedly as anyone else. But maturing in the years immediately after a world war and the Shoah, what was foremost was a vision of peace, a definitive elimination of the disasters just ended, and the restoration of the culture that had failed—or that had been kidnapped, rather, for evil purposes.

Reading was, first of all, a mode of acculturation, all the more so for an immigrant. It promised a way of learning whatever had to be learned, of absorbing its strangeness, of hoarding new expressions and puzzling out the direction from which they hit, the source of their appeal. The plot was words themselves, as changeable in context as the look of seductive models: film stars or singers who surprise each year with new face, coiffure, dress, character—even, it almost seems, body.

In his 1951 reissue of *Exile's Return*, Malcolm Cowley emphasizes Gertrude Stein's assertion that American writers like Hemingway, Dos Passos, and Fitzgerald, who made their mark in the postwar world of the 1920s, were a "lost generation." Kenneth Burke, for his part, talks of being "thirties minded." I don't know exactly when this generational calculus began to take hold, but, as Cowley observes, artists and critics felt they were being wrenched away from attachment to region or tradition, and often decided to live in exile during a "period of transition from values already fixed to values that had to be created."

Perhaps in some major urban centers the years after World War II were also marked by a generational self-consciousness. Much has been written about the "New York School," consisting not only of painters but also literary personalities often associated with the *Partisan Review*. It is clear from Cowley's lively account that, in the earlier period, artists who had not expatriated themselves to Paris habitually spent their winters in New York. A literary group committed to the "religion of art" could be found there, an odd assortment including, among many others, Allen Tate, Hart Crane, and Kenneth Burke. It featured political discussions, poetry parties, and Smith and Vassar girls (imitation Lady Brett Ashleys) "inundating" New York with talk of "our generation," in distinction from Cowley's "lost generation," yet determined to form attachments to and learn from the older men. Not without fierce intellectual quarrels, the participants made a front against the philistine "commodity culture" of America, and a great deal of literary passion and productivity went into small, transient magazines like *Broom*, *transition*, and *Secession*.

That was in the 1920s. My situation, arriving in New York in 1945, a boy just sixteen years old, was bound to be lonely. It was exciting only because of the wonder of finding myself among skyscrapers in a monster city. Immigrating from England, I knew no one except a few elderly relatives. Because of poverty, I could not take advantage of New York's cultural offerings except for an occasional movie at the Thalia or an oldie at the Museum of Modern Art. The city as such became imagination's focus, its blatant neon lights surprising me after years of a blacked-out England, and tall buildings with innumerable windows hinting at intimate dramas. No wonder Gassner's American theater anthology appealed tremendously.

As for the "celestial ennui of apartments": what was celestial about the roach-infested cubbyhole I lived in, an adolescent among three ancient (in my eyes) tenants sharing a railroad corridor leading to a small kitchen and grungy bathroom? Every night I had to fumigate against cockroaches and go to sleep in a mist of DDT.

I threw myself into books, first at Hunter College (which admitted male students to evening classes in order to accommodate the crush of veterans using the GI Bill), and then full time at Queens College. Even in graduate school at Yale my life was monastic, spent mainly reading and studying, with almost no community or peer group. Those I felt closest to, Kurt Weinberg, Konrad Bieber, and Ralph Freedman, were considerably older, having passed through the war.

Becoming a teacher, of course, and I forget how far down the line of that experience, my academic "cohort," as sociologists say (though we lacked, I think, till well into the 1960s, the wish to be defined as a generation, whether yuppie, or popping or rocking, or X-rated, or even having the consciousness we were anything special)—my cohort, then, began to read for the plot in a peculiar way. It wasn't the story-plot but the writer's own devices and manipulations. Fortified by Modernist literature, by the New Criticism too and its clean enthusiasm for experiments with literary form as a mode of discovery, the hot-button terms were technique, strategy, and stiffeners called paradox and irony. We indulged in the literary equivalent of war games. Eventually we came to resent such designs and turned into predeconstructionists who demystified every text, motivated by regret for our own (lost) spontaneity and sometimes by a self-righteousness borrowed from reigning literary pundits.

In my case, that stage was skipped. I was too grateful to Britain and America for hospitably taking me in to play those games. European stylistics, moreover, its immense respect for the evolution of the literary vernaculars, for the writer's struggle to find a symbiosis with an ever evolving language—as well as my instinctive Freudian feel for overdetermined meanings, all of which had to be given mental space—European stylistics, when practiced by masters like Auerbach and Spitzer, made such rhetorical counters as "irony," "paradox," even "ambiguity," except in William Empson's *Seven Types of Ambiguity*, pale reflections of a boundless and bountiful linguistic play. Nor did I fret much about issues of unity, coherence, and a so-called tough lyric grace.

Yet I did begin to read for the wound. That is, for some defining, too definitive, dubiously unifying imprint, incurred early or late, and returning sporadically to inflame and inspire, like a forgotten injury. Might a psychic mark of that kind have mysteriously strengthened the artist, as Edmund Wilson argued in *The Wound and the Bow*? Did such a mark become the artist's signature, or was it a peculiar, post-Romantic idea that the torment could have been self-inflicted, a sort of "I bleed, therefore I am," an emancipatory act of individuation as well as extreme sympathy for human suffering generally?

So in Coleridge's famous "Ancient Mariner," the protagonist's apparently gratuitous shooting of the albatross brings on all that consequence, including (today) the theoretical issue of how to understand the relation of unconscious motivation to the highly organized qualities of the work of art. Everything turns on the single one, the one singled out, who is simultaneously curse-wounded and blessed.

Wordsworth again was relevant. Individuation, in his experience, is not only the place of injury but that of virtual healing. Whatever trauma, in childhood or adulthood, raised his self-consciousness to apocalyptic pitch, so that he felt haunted by spots in the rural world that addressed him mutely like navel-points of the earth on which, once upon a time, ancient shrines were built, he credited the fearful as well as beautiful impact of

England's rural scenery with a "renovating virtue." What he came to call Nature (which, as a youngster, he had treated thoughtlessly and even with destructive abandon) was depicted in the autobiographical *Prelude* as a guiding, suffering, and sometimes frightening presence. He insisted that it had saved him from psychic and sensory fixations.

But in "Words and Wounds" (the last chapter of *Saving the Text*) I speculated that some anguish of socialization must have entered the process. Deeply shaming or embarrassing moments, accompanied by unforgivable words, words actually uttered, surely play their part, even when elided from consciousness. So that further words (poetry itself) must help to heal the wound words have made.

Psychoaesthetics suggests how integral artistic creation is to sanity by an imaginative engagement, a rite of passage during the turmoil leading beyond childhood and youth. I sensed in each work of fiction a potential threat of discontinuity, a charged, ecstatic or traumatic moment in disguise. At best, narrative embodied the mercy of time, a psychologically necessary extension allowing that moment to integrate. Yet time is not always merciful, and repetition may point to a compulsion, or, as in theater, an entrapment in what should have remained a trial incarnation.[50] Like Paul Ricoeur, I wanted to reconcile a hermeneutics of suspicion with an affirmative outcome that left the motivation to narrate intact.

As a phase, this soon became problematic. Was there any commonality between focusing on ordinary if troubling issues of socialization and my concentrating, as I did more and more, on the traumatic experience of the survivors of the camps? How could their experiences, which now came home to consciousness, be honestly listened to? What kind of secondary, or intellectual, witnessing was called for, and might testimonial narratives play a significant role in the life of the survivors as well as in the public pursuit of memorialization and human rights?

Perhaps, though, I remained more of a loner than this account implies. My turning to the interpretive daring of psychoanalysis and trauma studies, even if all this was not unusual, intimates a personal need. One pretends, retrospectively, to be part of a collective movement, less out of modesty than in order to think of oneself as having been at the crest of a gathering wave. There I hover still, as friends and colleagues die, disenchanted by the waning force of a once self-defining, now vague generation, whose coherence may never have existed except for the very branding it no longer acknowledges.

As a displaced child of Europe, what were my relations with German scholars, in particular, after I entered an academic career? (My friendships with researchers and academics from other countries, like Annette Wieviorka of the Centre Nationale de Recherche Scientifique, the French government-supported think tank, and Yannis Thanassekos of the Free University of Brussels and the Auschwitz Foundation, were focused almost entirely on developing video testimony projects. Later, an interest in German Jewish writers became the basis for a lasting friendship with Vivian Liska of the University of Antwerp, while memory studies and the personal warmth of

Relations with German scholars. Conversation with Hans-Robert Jauss.

Giovanna Franci and Daniela Carpi keep drawing me back to Italy.)[51]

In the beginning, I did not seek German contacts. I agreed to substitute for Paul de Man at Zürich, but precisely because it was not Germany. Nevertheless, already during that first Swiss visit in 1966–67, I accepted invitations by Peter Szondi to Berlin and by Hans Robert Jauss to Konstanz. Gradually friendships grew and my admiration for German scholarship increased, especially in the area of philosophical hermeneutics. I will provide some excerpts, as it were, from my visits to Germany.

There have been lasting contacts in Heidelberg with Horst and Margrit Meller, with Aleida and Jan Assmann (first in Heidelberg, then in Konstanz and Yale), with Anselm Haverkamp and Barbara Vinken. Anselm I had met in Konstanz, when he audited my guest seminar on contemporary American poetry. Much later, Aleida and he conspired to edit a Festschrift for me in Germany. It was a symbolic act motivated by the thought (or so I interpreted the gift) that "if Hartman had not been forced to leave this country, we would now be offering him such a volume."[52] The contributors were mainly their students, colleagues, and acquaintances. I was moved by that gesture; it represented a rising generation of German scholars free enough of guilt to assume, and creatively work through, a sense of responsibility for the past. The volume's introduction developed what the editors identified as my own concept of restitution: the effort to preserve and bring to scholarly attention the testimonial voice of Holocaust survivors.

There were other returns, all (I think) unavoidably symbolic, and sometimes that was uncomfortable as well as appreciated. Horst Meller organized a conference in Heidelberg circa 1985 on "Saving the Text," where I met the philosopher Hans-Georg Gadamer, over eighty but still spry. When the two Shakespeare Associations, which, like Germany itself, had split into East and West, decided to reunite in the early 1990s, I was asked to give the keynote address. A strange choice, since I was hardly a mainline scholar of Shakespeare. An occasion that gave me special pleasure was being asked by Winfried Menninghaus to deliver an anniversary talk in honor of Peter Szondi's founding of the Free University of Berlin's General and Comparative Literature Institute. I have often enjoyed the hospitality of the Einstein Forum in Berlin, as well as of the Zentrum für Literaturforschung under the guidance of Sigrid Weigel and Karl-Heinz Barck, and I also spent a few months at the Berlin *Wissenschaftskolleg*.

It was at the Kolleg that my presentation of Yale's video testimony project moved Wolfgang Mommsen (twin brother of the distinguished Holocaust historian Hans Mommsen and himself a historian of modern Germany) to question fiercely the value of such oral documentation. He did so, I believe, not out of any secret guilt—both Wolfgang and Hans have publicly admitted the shock of discovering at war's end that their historian father had been a fervent Nazi supporter and all that was implied by that—but precisely because their discovery had led the brothers to become "left-wing" scholars of the most troubled period of modern Germany, from nineteenth-century preludes to the Nazi disaster. I suspect the emotional side of oral testimony went against the decorum of the documentary history Wolfgang practiced. Had Saul Friedlander been present, he might have characterized

Wolfgang's outburst as a case of negative transference. (Wolfgang later sought me out to discuss the issue more calmly.) I do not discredit his sincerity, only the still widespread reluctance of some historians at that time to engage with oral history.

One of my earliest academic relationships in Germany was with Hans Robert Jauss. In his case, like de Man's, there was war damage in the form of a belated disclosure. Jauss, perhaps the most distinguished professor of Romance philology in Germany, a founder of the University of Konstanz, and an important player in "Reader Reception" theory, was identified in the late 1980s as a former officer in the Waffen-SS, which the Nuremberg Tribunal classified as a criminal organization. This outing occurred at the height of his reputation and just before his retirement. An unfailingly courteous person, with a somewhat military bearing, he had married a Jewish woman after the war; in his relation to me and other professorial guests he was always cordial and hospitable.

I had helped to invite him to Yale as a visiting professor, and he proved to be a demanding but very successful teacher with an immense literary knowledge and an exceptional clarity of exposition. The categories he invented or modified, such as "aesthetic experience," were used with both rigor and subtlety. As always, I admired the continental European ability to integrate philosophical and hermeneutic issues with literary studies. (Wolfgang Iser, in the "Anglistik" domain, whom I also saw often in both Konstanz and the States, shared that courage for grand literary theory.) But my purpose here is not to reduce a scholar's achievement to textbook phrases. It is to describe the past coming back with a vengeance, and, as with de Man, casting a shadow on an intellectual friendship.

Jauss initiated a correspondence after the news broke, seeking to explain his situation as a youngster during the Nazi era. We were finally able to have a face-to-face conversation about this in the fall of 1988. I had written him that such a talk was necessary, although he took umbrage at my request. He insisted that given our long friendship I should trust him. The following is the gist of our conversation recorded in a diary I kept at the time:

Long delayed conversation. Jauss's claim of being naive about the Nazi persecution of the Jews while attending an international summer camp in France just before the war. He remembers his puzzlement when a Dutch Jewish girl says: Should you be sitting with me? and he even remembers the girl's name. He joins the Waffen-SS in October 1939, like a number of his classmates, to escape labor service and make sure he would receive the "Abitur" [the matriculation certificate necessary to go from High School to University]. His parents were no Nazis yet did not interfere with his decision. He himself, a recruit of the *Hitler Jugend*, never became a member of the Party.

His provincial town escaped participating in a *Kristallnacht* type of action. He saw the posted *Stürmer* [a viciously antisemitic newspaper displayed in public places] but considered it to be the expression of a small and vulgar element. Of his classmates only a handful returned from combat. What war fever he felt vanished when the first comrade fell at his side. His aim throughout the war was to have as many as possible under his command return safely. [Jauss served as the commander of a unit on the Russian front.]

When interrogated in the internment camp, where he was held two years before being pronounced clean, and asked if he had witnessed any atrocities, such as Jews or Russian soldiers being murdered by the SS, he answered that, to the contrary, his only such experience was of the SS being butchered by the Russians. During military service he was at one point assigned to lead a contingent of foreign volunteers, first Dutch, then French. He knew that other groups of the SS did dirty work ("schmutzige Arbeit") but did not see any of it nor was his unit ever involved.

I asked him directly why he had not told me or others about that part of his life. He said he had participated in a 1972 seminar on the collective memory with Professor Luhmann, in which he mentioned his Waffen-SS career. He had also let it be known that he should not be given important administrative positions. However, he seemed uncomfortable with this question. "You haven't told me about your experiences either," he added, as if there was a parallel. He used the word *pudeur* to describe his attitude, and said he had to put that period—for which he admitted guilt, or rather a collective "Haftung"—behind him, marrying a woman of Jewish descent, whom he had told about the Waffen-SS, and who had accepted him. She advised him not to let her family know. But some ten years ago his brother-in-law learnt about it, urged Helga to leave him, and never saw him again ("Er hat das Tischtuch zerissen").

What, in any case, should he have done with such a knowledge burden? he suddenly asked. I sensed in all this a hurt pride; there was some facial trembling. I told him I felt I had to be informed, but not in order to pass judgment at this point. He then added that an Israeli historian had asked to join him for a glass of wine, in order, it turned out, to quiz him as a valuable observer. The historian offered not to make use of his statements; but Jauss, since he had not done anything to incur personal guilt, gave him permission.

I suggested it might be good for him to write about his war experiences rather than leave the account to others. Now that a new situation had been created by the public disclosure, everything he had put behind him was again before him. His literary experience would surely help in this task; yet I failed to glimpse that in the formal and apologetic style he was still using with me. Could he drop the courtesy formulas and his humanistic epistolary manner, although I had no reason to doubt the real sadness behind such formal distinctions as: "If you cannot accept me any longer as a friend, I would still like to be a colleague"?

Autobiography, he indicated, was not his mode. While I understood this, I continued to feel his resentment that long-time friends would not accept him as before, despite his trustworthy postwar career. It was certainly difficult that he should have to prove himself, as if his postwar life and scholarly contribution were not persuasive enough. Had his career been less stellar, the issue, publicly at least, would have been moot.

The next day he sought me out to say: I had the impression last night that you wanted from me the conversation you did not have with Paul de Man.

What kind of Jewishness?

I turn once more, in conclusion, to Judaic studies. That commitment, as I have said, matured slowly and did not find a chance to be creative until 1980—except for fledgling attempts to write poetry. I want to look again at what happened to and within me. Was my change highly individual, even idiosyncratic, in the sense of being typical only of a displaced child, or does it represent a contemporary type of personal evolution?

I lack childhood associations with prayer services or communal ceremonies. To this day I can't sit in a synagogue for very long, and envy Renée's careful and happy participation. While she *davens* with patience and warmth, I fidget. After coming to America, Renée soon left the strictly religious life with her orthodox relatives in Williamsburg, but one thing she remembers greatly enjoying there, all the more so because she did not have it as a child in the home of deaf parents: the table hymns (*zemirot*) sung especially at the festive meal that welcomes the Sabbath. I too enjoy that singing, but cannot lose myself in it. I want to understand better what is being read, sung, and prayed, and wander over the pages of the *Siddur* with a critical eye, trying to become interested, finding food for thought in certain ritual formulas, regretting the lack of poetry in many of the translations—in short, relying on my intellect to engage the emotions. Profane thoughts are not the trouble, they rarely distract me; it is the words of the prayers themselves, or aspects of the ritual, like swaddling and unswaddling the Torah scrolls, that make me at once reflective and frustrated. There is considerable anguish in knowing how excluded I am from an emotional identification with religious rituals.

Those rituals, and idioms, need respect for their strangeness. They ask to be restored to some "ur" meaning—bare, essential, existential. I try to become the child I never was, or rather a poet who responds to some original, faint residue, like a remembered scent that comes to you revisiting a city you have known in bygone days. Listening to the prayers of the congregation a feeling rises that here, even if the meaning remains half-hidden, are heartfelt cries that need the unison of a community to be heard. Yet I hear only the void shouting back.

Sometimes I am guided by what William Blake called a "Memorable Fancy." He can imagine himself dining with Isaiah and Ezekiel, or talking with Milton and Shakespeare. I regret a lost *chevra*, the company of German Jewish scholars forced into exile. Some, like Gershom Scholem, Ernst Simon, Hannah Arendt, and A. J. Heschel, I still met fleetingly; others, like Martin Buber, Hugo Bergmann, and Nahum Glatzer, I knew only through their books. (I continue to treasure *Sendung und Schicksal*, the reader of Jewish sources Glatzer edited with Ludwig Strauss in the early 1930s, picked up secondhand in Tel-Aviv on my first visit there in July 1952.) There is no wish to identify with them, to imitate or directly emulate: simply to preserve a measure of their greatness. In the absence of father and grandfather, indeed all family except a mother I had grown apart from after close to seven years of separation, I adopted myself out to words blowing in the wind and insights that detached themselves from what I read promiscuously in the little tomes of the Schocken Verlag or whatever book I carried about like a talisman.

By now you may be reminded of a cliché that contains a lot of truth. Was I making the book, or the aura of great books, my homeland? But the curious fact is I did not feel like an exile. I was the Unexile. Through my twofold displacement I eventually fell into the category of what Philip Rieff once named a "Jew of culture" and Amos Oz a "Jew, but not of the Synagogue." I was devoted to Judaism yet not very observant, and so a person for whom, when it came to literature or the arts, no bright dividing line separated Jewish and non-Jewish, or sacred and secular. Nor was I prejudiced against the classics of my mother tongue. Studying German Romanticism I felt as totally at home with Hölderlin and Goethe as with Wordsworth and Keats. Of course I realized that great writers were not exempt from being misappropriated and propagandized, yet such theft or misprision simply increased the ante: freedom of interpretation should not lead to ideologically induced distortions. These distortions were a good reason for cultivating interpretation theory as a historical and disciplinary field essential to the humanities.

I had no deliberate return, then, to Judaism. Brought up with the barest formal or family-based knowledge of the tradition, I became a raider and explorer. I did not have to break away in order to return and find myself. Midrash and other aspects of Judaism opened their peculiar riches through a belated intellectual acquisition.

Which leads me to think again of my one direct scholarly (rather than organizational) effort in the area of Judaic

studies. I initiated a semester's teaching at the
Hebrew University's English department in the
fall of 1958. Harold Bloom and I split a year,
each offering a semester course. Those few months in
Israel gave me the opportunity to attend the Midrash
classes of Nehama Leibowitz. My knowledge of Hebrew
at that time was (and, alas, remains) minimal, though I
sense a magic in its strange alphabet whenever I turn to
the Hebrew Bible. Its script, like stony relics of a distant
civilization, has the aura of an elemental simplicity. In
contrast, the rich, elliptical outgrowth of midrashic divi-
nations comforts like desert flowers after the rains.

From inauspicious beginnings like these came an avid if
sporadic reading of Midrash, mainly in English and German. At Yale, I proposed an annual conference celebrat-
ing May Day as Midrash Day. (The idea had a longevity
of two years.) When Sanford Budick of the Hebrew University founded an Institute for Literary Studies circa
1980 and invited me to help inaugurate it, I suggested
its first year should be devoted to the midrashic mode of
interpretation. From that came our jointly edited volume,
Midrash and Literature (1986).

Can Midrash be fruitful for modern literary interpretation? Like deconstruction, it makes literary studies more
thoughtful. I look beyond the deliberately nonhistorical
side of deconstruction and allow myself the conclusion:
"Ask not what deconstruction can do for Midrash, ask
what Midrash can do for deconstruction." I glimpse an
affinity between Derrida's playfulness in *Glas* and the
surprising liberality, the multivocality of *midrash agga-
dah*, which is less closely tied to legal issues than *midrash
halakhah*.

149

It is not out of the question that midrashic methods could intrigue those interested in both formal hermeneutics and the practice of interpretation generally. An immersion in that textual corpus is necessary, no doubt, before Midrash can influence contemporary practice. Already, however, the intensity and speculative daring of contemporary readings presenting themselves as purely or defiantly secular recall an older religious practice. Except that religious types of reading stick to the text at all costs, so that everyone can follow, hold on, and argue by citing a proof verse or proffering a "davar acher" (another word, i.e., meaning), always returning to the passage in question and the "tribunal of the court here below" if there is disagreement with a peculiar application or an unacceptable flight of fancy. All I can do, since I have not undergone a Midrash immersion long enough, is to convey my personal conviction that this tradition of Scriptural exegesis, which has remained nearly invisible in literary circles, is worth exploring and may even bring back some of the laity we have lost.

If for non-Jewish readers I opened a chink into the sacred wood, or rather jungle, of Midrash, it was also in the hope of helping to dispel a deadly slander: that Judaism is a religion marked by a legalistic and materialistic literalism. There was another benefit too. Midrash showed that commentary could be a form of literature. In preserving the Hebrew Bible, a text open to centuries of votive offerings, endlessly consumed and renewed by being cited, Midrash remains the literature of orthodox Jews, an extraordinary blend of intellectual and imaginative, legal and inventive thought. Emmanuel Levinas, too, has continued that fruitful if complex exploration.

In the Talmud's formative period, the freedom and range of interpretive moves excluded the possibility of a strict literalism, even while Jewish patristics adhere to the exact words of a consecrated text. Those words are preserved unaltered despite their overt or subtle contradictions. The danger that a single fixed interpretation would replace the text is averted by reporting, in abbreviated form, the disputations and minority opinions of the early rabbis. Through certain techniques of recombination and even permutation, moreover, the sacred text becomes a kind of primal verbal matter that can be aurally reshaped by the faithful interpreter.

Halakhic (law-finding) Midrash can disconcert by its minutiae and *pilpul* pickiness. The ingenuity shown the biblical text is also turned toward the Talmudic text by sifting every legal rule for its rationale. Even this punctilio is addictive, however: not only because it trains the mind to seek out the reasoning behind every pronouncement but because it gives the modern reader the impression, received from scientific inquiry generally, that there is a deep concatenation at work, that the Talmud has something of the intricacy of what underlies nature's phenomena.

Looking across the writing, then, done over some fifty years, I can see how important the call of literature was: how it sustained both a verbal discipline and an imaginative hope. It did not foster, though it might have, the solipsism of a youngster who grew up without a family and depended on the kindness of strangers. Instead, the idea of literature and that of community came together in a turn to teaching as mutual learning. This was the ideal implicit in the interpretive study of consecrated texts, an animated sharing not basically different from what I later recognized as the spirit of Midrash. Literature became secular Scripture and literary commentary secular Midrash.[53]

A persistent love for poetry. My greatest pleasure, though, was tempting the Muse. I wanted to write beyond the middle style. Like the Romantics, I was unwilling to give up a visionary kind of verse, even if it meant raiding a sacred treasure and risking profanation or pastiche. Yehuda Halevy's poetry made me aware of the power of pastiche, of integrated if displaced biblical phrases, and this influenced my fledgling poetic ventures. The Song of Songs was the model that justified the sacred dictions in Halevy's love songs from exile. But given my distinctly secular subject matter, I tried to communicate a sense of the disparity of diction and content, even a hint of profanation, through a *contrafactura* method strangely similar to how John Barth defined metafiction: "cool riffs on the classical tune."

Eventually I started and never sustained a long poem in which Spenser, Shelley, the masters of Midrash, and God knows who else kept me aloft. The poem's allegory represented those who "in the wide deep wandering are" and whose path crossed mine. That wandering continues, with poetic moments surprising me like markers in a mist.

Why, despite the prosaic nature of the critical act and pressures coming from political and social problems that seem to increase daily have I not given up thinking and writing about poetry, and especially Romantic poetry? On the verge of retirement, ten years ago, I looked forward to devoting myself to the study of Hebrew Scripture, its commentators, and German Jewish writing in the time between the First World War and the Shoah. It did not happen. I could not close my Keats, Wordsworth, Blake, or Shakespeare. Or, for that matter, Thoreau and Whitman, or the Wallace Stevens who said that the great poems of heaven and hell had been written but the great poem of earth was still to come.

My adherence to the poets and a poetic kind of thinking has a realistic base. There is a contest between poetry and divinity, between those subsuming passions. The history of religion and religious politics has provided many Great Awakenings, many self-anointed prophets and redeemers with enormous influence and often catastrophic consequences. This eternal return of religion, or what Matthew Arnold (adapting the Saint-Simonian view of history as cyclical) named epochs of concentration, cannot be ignored. Northrop Frye's last chapter in his *The Secular Scripture* is "The Recovery of Myth." The conviction has formed in me that religion is sustained by ritual and romance, intensely imaginative conceptions, but these are too often skeletalized by a dogmatic theology or exploited by extreme sectarian politics. From that perspective the mental fight of the Romantic poets, in particular, is exemplary. When I read Keats's unfinished *Hyperions*, I glimpse the remarkable drama of a poet "shamed by the knowledge that the gods are born once more of him, that great poetry must survive, if at all, in a cockney's breast." Who was more secular than Keats? Yet he had to approach the great poem of earth through what he once called a "load of immortality."

Toward the end of this academic tale I append verses from *Akiba's Children*. Belated, and indebted to visionary imagery, they remain a post-Romantic fragment.

Mariner's Song

After He had maimed the dragon deep
And throned us in new limbs of everlasting,
Opening to fable the mortal stars:
We wept praises and harped the flood
    of His word.
Our tears might have filled an ocean,
Our blood a sea.
We followed or wantoned before Him:
He was our serpent, flexible and brazen,
On His broad back we crossed the seas
Or stood precipitously between worlds.
Come now, with a staunch heart, a steady
    love,
Redeem His river-bones from Egypt,
Fetch home His visions, and out of His grave
Make a vineyard to plant the voice
    of the dove.

Concluding thoughts on friendship, teaching, aging, the age, and . . . memoirizing.

Double trouble digits. I finish my account having reached 77. The numbers are against me. Every day, it seems, I have to fight to prevent isolating myself from terrible news that comes unbidden, especially via the media. Also to keep up an intellectual curiosity that remains strong, yet not as strong as before. I open the morning paper listlessly or anxiously. Would one continue to read if everything read were bad news?

A principle of hope still lurks somewhere. There was a time when I could say, with Victor Hugo, "J'admire tout, comme une bête." In my case, it was astonishment rather than admiration and included being surprised when certain things failed to surprise. It was up to me to detox myself by an intellectual follow-up. One thing has not changed: my thought, compared to that of more genial writers, totters like an infant from the sheltering hands of one parent-idea to the other, while they are Café Non-Stop.

Until recently I was moved only abstractly by the old man (avatar of the Wandering Jew) in one of Chaucer's *Canterbury Tales* who tells the rowdies seeking in a parody of chivalric quests to get rid of "that villain death": "I knock with my staff on the earth, both early and late, pleading: 'Dear mother, let me in!'" Yet even today, more attuned to his plea, I feel no urgency to be justified in the manner of Rousseau. This does not imply I am unaware of my limits, and especially of a hesitation to expend myself in love or hate.

I have remained friends with my closest students. My affection for them, and even now for many teachers and students I encounter through the lectures and public seminars I still like to give, is surely a kind of love. But I have not harbored the wish to create a following. The give and take of a seminar discussion was always a real pleasure, and so the noticeably brilliant individual seemed only as important as a collective reading effort that produced insights on the part of even the less brilliant. Was I too distancing at times? It is possible; having had to bring myself up, I attribute a significant measure of autonomy to others, dislike any sort of intellectual coercion, and may have been, at times, a "lazy-faire" teacher and mentor.[54]

I find that those who study with me respond to three aspects of teaching. The first, and most important, is their sense that what we are jointly discovering is really there, based on the text, and probatively so. All teacher-interpreters like to think their reading is the correct or significant one. But persuasion, if it happens, should come from respecting a process that involves returning to the words on the page, however speculative the discussion becomes, however adventurous our byways.

The second aspect, not unrelated, is that I try to listen to each idea the text elicits in the student and pursue it to some extent even when it seems outlandish. My favorite cartoon illustrating the necessity of this comes from the *New Yorker* and shows a British pub in which a chap is looking suspiciously at his glass of beer. British pubs usually have a dartboard for entertainment, and quite conspicuously a dart is stuck in the puzzled drinker's head. So we explore a feeling or observation that should not be immediately rejected: it may have been displaced, joined to a falsely located source.

To define the third aspect I call on Coleridge's help. He attributed a special quality to poetry. Poetry, he said, was a species of composition whose object is immediate pleasure rather than truth (truth being the immediate as well as ultimate object of science), and in which that pleasure—of the poem as a whole—is compatible with a distinct gratification derived from each component part. I therefore ask those who study with me to think of the literary artifact as a maze, which should have one way through (call it the truth or validity), but the wandering about, the errancy, is legitimate, and what is found on the way to the way out, even if not relevant for resolving a particular amazement, should remain intriguing rather than negligible.

No wonder he is a slow reader, you think. A seminar I used to give on "Interpretation: Theory and Practice" sometimes began with the first line of Wordsworth's "Strange fits of passion I have known" and a warning that it might take the greater part of our opening session to unpack that line. I would progress as slowly as the horse in that poem, which seems to have entered the dream world of its rider. I won't impose my reading here except to say it asked where in this lyric the fit of passion was to be found, a question that cannot be followed through without considering the connotations of "fits" and the semantic field of "passion."

What haunts a memoir that does not have the excuse of a significant personal conversion, revelation, exculpation, is the nexus of the life and the work. I strive to discover that link even if it proves to be reductive. Without such a link, is there realism? Living so long in the ambience of the academy, I am tempted to define the humanist's lack of realism as coming from the substitution of the university for the universe and too often accepting its gossipy judgments as godly. But do not all of us have an encompassment of this kind? Every new movement that speaks for realism accuses the preceding one of evasion and abstractness—of not being in touch or turning a blind eye to the world. We live within not only a societal but also a nonhuman surround, within the largeness and largesse of the cosmos, and often have difficulty humanizing ourselves.

In this commitment of the autobiographer to realism, an unceasing tension prevails between "you shall tell" and "let it remain in you." Perhaps, then, as Oscar Wilde claimed, literary criticism is the only civilized form of autobiography. The theater of the mind plays out a tension between reticence and self-revelation.

The link with realism, the primary concern of the finding mind—and hardly bearable without wit and improvisation—points to the family before engaging the issue of further social contexts. When, in adolescence, a youngster erupting in blind anger swears at a parent, not just with ordinary but with violently obscene words (even if ignorant of their literal meaning), something dies. A parent must agree to suffer this kind of humiliation, this pseudodeath. The breach it makes, in both child and parent, is that of a necessary disenchantment, of being forced to pass, even and once more as an adult, from childhood to adulthood. As a sin against time and process that psychic wound is hard to heal. Did the child sense the breach to come and test it prematurely? Is it not really accusing the parent of hypocrisy, of pretending the breach doesn't yet exist, although the "yet" is all that stands in the way, and the "not yet!" the prohibition, is what fuels the explosive words? Have these and similar moments entered my concern with words and wounds?

Renée writes in a poem: "The ways to truth are crooked." Then also: "The ways to God are bloody." Her poem, a protest, concludes with the recognition that she must be her own child and organize her own innocence. This seems like an accusation, of God, of parents, for their failed protection. But the poem is also, as she then sees, and crying sees, a gift to her parents, a kaddish despite the bitter words. They were not there to be questioned. Renée's very writing of poetry, often in her mother tongue, is associated with wishing to merit and perpetuate father and mother, almost lost to remembrance because vanishing so early in her life during the Holocaust.

When in the mood prompting these pages I dip into my sporadic, diarylike notebooks, I realize how much has been omitted, then as now. What remains are scraps and scribbles about the inner life, occasional responses to family relations, scholarly debates, travels. I do not say enough, for example, about sometimes intense conversations, with Larry Langer, James Young, and Saul Friedlander on responses to the Holocaust, with Richard Bernstein on political philosophy, with Leslie Brisman and Paul Fry on Wordsworth, with Carolin Emcke on witnessing and reportage, with Helen Elam, Frances Ferguson, Elizabeth Freund, Shira Wolosky, and Kevis Goodman about our mutual wish to keep the study of poetry as an absorbing and competitive discipline, and discussions with many other colleagues here and abroad.

I do not say enough about numerous visits to Israel beginning as early as the summer of 1952, of how deeply the landscape and the friendships affected me.[55] To be obliged to assert that Israel has the right to exist is deeply offensive: it should not have to be said. One lives with a critical mind, one remains a thinking, watchful person, but on that matter there is no ambivalence in me. I think of the hope, at the same time, scuttled again and again, of brotherly peoples living together in amity. Sorrow takes hold when I see the necessity for self-defense becoming the mother of so much suffering. Yet what I feel I can express only in poetry, as if a univocal meaning could not surface. "Fumes of passion, exhaust of too much love. . . .

Crying from the ground, the blood of so many / Who can hear?" Boehme's aphorism comes to mind as he thinks of an angry God: "Love is wrath quenched."

Where in my account is the poet-patriot and journalist Haim Gouri, whose three-part documentary film centering on the Holocaust was so important for me? Where my conversations, political and literary, with Yaron and Sidra Ezrahi?[56]

A great deal of the precise impact of these conversations, conferences, incidents, is lost. In general, I looked too much toward the future, and resisting the spell of visuality turned both from mobilizing that enchantment and from its more utilitarian aspect as a fixative of exemplary detail.

I gave up photography, not wanting to dwell on capturing images but rather to absorb and "develop" them by an energy coming from my own thoughts. (I recall a remark of Wordsworth's that once struck me as peculiar, when he refused to assign "I wandered lonely as a cloud" to the category of "Poems of the Imagination." The inspiration behind the poem, he said, was influenced too much by the "ocular spectrum.") Also from early on I disliked learning poetry by heart, fearing its mnemonic imprint would become mechanical. By reading poetry I wanted to unlock the poetry within me. While an auditory intensity enabled me to hear words within words, and surface their virtual puns or other forms of sound-reasoning, I could never really fit the episodic event, whether visual or verbal, and thrown up and against me by life, into an accommodating narrative frame. As an epigraph to one of the final chapters of *The Unmediated Vision*, I chose Rilke's "I have no roof over my head, and it rains into my eyes."

Even now perceptions continue to startle, and while I do sometimes compose them into mental snapshots, the two senses of "seeing"—sight and understanding—drift ever further apart and do not let me rest.

During my lifetime certain changes beyond anyone's control have altered the sensory milieu. Some are momentous, yet one learns to be cautious about applying the language of crisis. Has there been a general desensitization? Jan Kott, the dramaturg, remarks that contemporary audiences view cruelty and slaughter on the stage more calmly than those of a century ago. Or, could one have anticipated, after the Holocaust, a head of state who speaks, as the president of Iran has recently done, of wanting to annihilate another nation-state? But many of the changes I am thinking of are more commonplace, though still related to the increasing decibels of the media.

I did not see a single movie before the age of nine. For all my adolescent years, until living in New York, the movies remained a special treat, a near-festive occasion like someone's birthday. My notebooks, especially from the 1960s until I abandoned them, are full of comments centering on (mainly) foreign films. Now, every day, every hour, I can surf several channels as well as visit the Big Screen. The result is indifference to what used to be a magical occasion, a typical blunting toward the often frenetic realism of the medium, so that little of an early eagerness is left. Instead, there is a frustrated voyeurism and an impotent desire to intervene. Am I approaching the condition of Watanabe-san, the dying bureaucrat in Kurosawa's *Ikiru*? I am moved by that film's portraiture, its visual scripting of every melodramatic gesture and guttural characterization.

Life is mimicry, consciously or not, of a preordained ritual pattern. How to break through, and make that breakthrough an achievement, not only in itself but as a memory that can be transmitted and honored collectively, yet one that retains its individual imprint, its very human nuances? Assuring, as in Kurosawa's *Ikiru*, the construction of a children's playground, preventing it being aborted by deadly, paper-pushing bureaucrats who embody the social and sacred rituals that have deformed them, is something of a triumph, although a triumph always threatened, as in Kurosawa's film, by trivialization and denigration. It is as sublime in its way as Cleopatra's suicide. Thomas Mann points out that Cleopatra's choosing to die by applying an asp to her breast is not a gesture of defeat but of transcendence, of a ritual identification with the goddess Isis. Memorable, and again a completion of sorts.

Like everyone else in this Western society, I live in a world at once unreal and too real. Soon everything will not only be interrupted by ads but will itself be an ad. The ultimate TV show, I fantasize, the ultimate commodity culture, may feature ads instead of the feature, and where such ads used to be, nostalgic fragments of a feature. I already cull sporadic insights about the contemporary world from a film's glossy and accelerating displays of the human condition, displays that allow less and less time for reflection, and I understand why so many are enticed by video games, especially interactive ones like the Sim series. Yet their vis-à-vis, their "You," climaxing as YouTube and its mirror-image celebration by *Time* magazine's 2006

"Person of the Year" cover, is the ultimate, if interactive, narcissism.

The theater, at least, with actors embarrassingly present rather than body doubles, and sustaining a risky role closer to real time, still comes home to me. As does the exquisite unreality, the preternatural flex of body and voice in ballet and opera.

The Modernist movement in art understood that an overdose of realism would damage our sense of reality. Techniques of estrangement were introduced as a countermeasure. Today the anime holds its own against the sensory assault of the Big Reality Movie precisely by a degree of abstraction and artifice achieved through the residual or deliberate awkwardness of its figures. Yet the apparent ease with which the animator can bring morphing fantasies to the screen simply produces a new type of phantomization. A previous mode of reality-testing—the self-questioning of art, the disturbance by art of its own magic—loses its effectiveness when the medium becomes a closed circuit of interactive and manipulated moves.

Even the process of mediation is standardized when an electronic and digital era gives it over to mechanism and technology. We seek a default position for everything. In an eloquent manifesto-fantasy by Tiziano Scarpa called "Pluriverse," which celebrates the art of the video game, I read: "Everything is middleware. Everything is a mediation between two software programs that apparently do not communicate with each other. The bridge between two banks is middleware. The translation of a haiku into Yeruba is middleware. . . . The amniotic fluid is middleware. The umbilical cord is middleware. Words are middleware. From today, with the password we will shortly give you, it is possible to enter Pluriverse and play anything. The Network has finally been created."

Mediation, once a material or spiritual reality principle, turns into a gaming competition leading to versions seeking an unlimited virtual domain. Consequently the programmer, *magister ludi* or demiurge, remains frigid. His interactive universes implode, collapse into each other, and this leads to the following self-indictment of the middleware genius. "You've created chaos in order to live in peace. You sit calmly in the eye of the cyclone while all around you the storm is raging."[57]

I fear this disconnect and apathy; I fear it not only in the younger generation but also in myself. A split is being created by this habituation through technology. Unmoved movers, we experience a compensatory emotional reflex, the very opposite of impassibility. It often shows itself as a very passionate, personal, and personalistic theology. The result may well be an even more intractable divide in the area of religious feelings.

Media are not mediations. The discontinuities they remove, and the apparently transparent or faultless pathways they create, cannot resolve existential human problems, persistent social conflicts. Mediation involves a risky engagement, and the likelihood, to which a ritual repetition testifies, of periodic anxiety, dearth, death, and disaster, of having to deal again and again with failure, rejection, singularity. The stakes are high, and the word retains a religious resonance. I can only hope that the response of the technological genius to his self-generated accusation does not fully characterize what I too may have transmitted in this memoir: "I programmed my desperate happiness. My serene and eternal discontent."

ERICH AUERBACH AT YALE

"The earth itself must now be the scholar's home; it can no longer be the nation."—PHILOLOGY OF WORLD LITERATURE

What I have to offer lies in the shadowy past of personal memory.[1] But it is refreshed by a conviction of the importance of the scholar we are considering. His exemplary status is so much clearer to me now than when I came to know him at Yale.

I am not sure why a casual reference to Erich Auerbach stayed with me, after hearing his name mentioned in Yale's graduate school. It was in a seminar given by René Wellek, whose erudition was overwhelming. Wellek's seminars seemed to consist of an endless roll call of names and books, accompanied by pithy judgments. He was a living *catalogue raisonné*. I had enthusiastically registered for two of his courses in 1949, my first year of study, one on the history of criticism, the other, obligatory, on literary theory. I remember Wellek praising, though in measured tones, a book by Erich Auerbach called *Mimesis*.

I was delighted by *Mimesis* as by a first-rate historical novel. Its extraordinary *explications de texte* opened my fact-weary eyes to the way detail, pregnant and more than pregnant, could be handled. Ah, those wondrous long German sentences, slowly unfolding by a method that never lost sight of the introductory and paradigmatic literary passage as it progressed to related excerpts and astonishingly large observations. And the magical matching up of exotic grammatical or rhetorical schemes, like parataxis and hypotaxis, with an author's social situation. I became more than a New Critic on the spot, without even knowing at that time quite what the New Criticism was—immunized by Auerbach's personal mastery of the very different and much older tradition of Romance stylistics.

It is true, being young, that I was searching for a more than arbitrary discipline, a scientific rigor to persuade me of the value of my impressions. And it is also true that Auerbach's opening chapter on Homer and the Bible, or rather the Book of Genesis, seduced me by something in addition to its precision: by its daring, as well as *esprit de finesse*. I did not immediately recognize that it was indebted to a polemical context. What I perceived was a generous conception of the unity of European literature, shaped by its capacity to absorb the *imaginaires* of two very different civilizations.[2]

I did eventually understand how German Classical scholarship, wishing to hold fast to Winckelmann's "Edle Einfalt und stille Grösse" (noble simplicity and quiet grandeur) limited even Auerbach's view of Homer. His unthreatening contrast, moreover, of those founding literary documents was deeply instructive in the wake of a traumatic period in which German scholarship had been totally politicized. Only a so-called Aryan canon was acknowledged; Judaic sources—modern authors such as Heine as well as nearly two millennia of Jewish biblical exegesis—were exorcized. Official propaganda also bad-mouthed—except when *raison d'état* masked the hostility—Romance literature's influences on "Nordic" German culture.

Later, when I read E. R. Curtius's magisterial work *European Literature and the Latin Middle Ages*, I got an inkling of how it too restored the larger integrity of the European canon by stressing "Romania"—and Goethe even more than Dante—as heroic conduit and intermediary. Leo Spitzer became the third in this trinity of restorative scholars; had I known Spanish and Italian better, there would have been others.

But I am getting ahead of myself. Though a refugee, entering graduate studies when barely twenty, I had only a vague knowledge of the Nazi culture war and the deadly opportunism of those whom Max Weinrich called "Hitler's professors." The evil fate I had escaped was shrouded in the mystery of iniquity. Even had I known more at that point, how could it possibly have tainted or modified my acceptance of Hölderlin, Hegel, Schiller, Novalis, Mörike, Rilke—the poetry, fiction, and essays I read with an immediate, fascinated appreciation? As I confessed in the preface to my thesis, published as *The Unmediated Vision*, I had fallen from innocence by eating of the tree of academic knowledge, but there were more apples to be eaten. Nor did my teachers in graduate school talk about either the war or the Holocaust. There was a flight from culture politics that intensified in the McCarthy era of the postwar 1940s and early 1950s.

Despite admiring Wellek's massive and broadly European erudition, I kept believing in the artist's capacity to experience life in its immediacy, or—a formula I learned from Hegel—to draw a new immediacy out of the multiple antithetical mediations that burdened individuality and originality. Auerbach became a Romantic in my eyes: he too transmuted learning into "the breath and finer spirit of all knowledge" (Wordsworth). *The Unmediated Vision* prefaced each chapter, as *Mimesis* had done, with a passage that served as a springboard to an author's entire oeuvre. To a somewhat skeptical Wellek asking me to justify my method and the four modern poets I had selected, I explained, making a virtue out of naïveté, that its aim was to present an inductive model for studying *any* literary work.

Less than a year after I first heard of Auerbach, he took a permanent position at Yale. By 1950, the concept of the Baroque, and the value of period terms generally, had become a hot topic, at least in comparative literature, partly because of Wellek, who defended their viability against Arthur Lovejoy, a founder of the "History of Ideas," who had attacked the imprecise, multifarious nature of such ordering concepts; it was Auerbach's seminar on the Baroque I attended.

For Wellek, period concepts were important because of a concern that nationalism, together with the cultural relativism to which it was reacting, would destroy the ideal premise of a larger, multinational unity that inspired scholarly inquiry and had helped to make the era of modern criticism possible. Period terms were a modest, heuristic way of demonstrating a richly inclusive rather than an abstract type of unity. It characterized the coexistence of many cultural phenomena within a major constellation of tendencies in search of a name. Auerbach, of course, practicing an urbane, undogmatic Marxism, took the pattern of a unified development characterizing European history more from social and economic realities.

Not unexpectedly, he began his seminar with Dante, and it soon became clear he was not really interested in period schematization. With finely chiseled voice he read this or that Dante extract aloud, and then . . . ruminated. Some students, coming from English, a discipline that at Yale marched its candidates from text to text with conquering pace, were disappointed. I felt privileged to overhear a truly literary scholar, with a "Feinschmecker" ingredient, freely rehearsing an incredible wealth of knowledge, which the verses he turned over in his mind confirmed or resisted. Even the rejects of his allusions were to me a "salon des réfusés."

My term paper for the course was on Maurice Scève's *Délie*, and it neglected the dixaines as love poems while analyzing innovative stylistic features that might fit into some definition of the Baroque. Auerbach was pleased, but he did allow himself to remark that perhaps one had to have more life experience to deal also with "amour passion." It is quite true, as I think back on it, that when I talked then about the immediacy of life, it meant a talent for pattern perception that was much more acute in my makeup, I might even say pure, than any other form of knowledge.

One felt that Auerbach as teacher was not entirely at home in the American classroom. I think it was he who told me the anecdote of a concert violinist, a refugee like himself, who complained that in America his violin emitted a different tone. Leo Spitzer too grumbled that he was "echolos," according to Henri Peyre, long-time head of Yale's French department.[3] But shyness kept me from talking with Auerbach, except in the classroom, or briefly on the occasion of visiting lectures by dignitaries. In those hierarchic days, such events took place in room 211 of Yale's Hall of Graduate Studies, with its rich wood paneling and imposing portraits of elders who still presided over the spirit of the place, and there all the senior professors sat at the front in one solemn phalanx. It did not inspire easy conversation.

My relationship to Auerbach changed when I started teaching at Yale in 1955, after a two-year, involuntary stint in the U.S. army. Auerbach invited me for a *gemütlich* conversation every fortnight. Frau Auerbach served tea, always asking whether I would like a drop of rum to go with it, and then withdrew. In the mid-1950s, the reputation of the Metaphysical poets, such as Donne, Herbert, Traherne, and Marvell, was still at its height, and Auerbach, somewhat mystified, asked me to read some of their poems with him.

Needless to say, I learned more from him than he from me. He suggested, for example, that Donne's strange and powerful "Anniversaries"—which magnified the death of Elizabeth Drew so much that his contemporary Ben Jonson accused him of blasphemy because of poetical conceits comparing the loss of this young girl in terms taken from the death and ascension of the Virgin—Auerbach surmised that Donne, full of curious learning as he was, might rather have been inspired by Sapientia or even the Shechinah, female figures of the Wisdom that dwelled with God from the beginning, and whose divinity and devotional importance were developed by medieval mystical traditions from a mention in the biblical book of Proverbs. He also talked of his research on the progress of medieval Latin as a literary language. He said his aim was to make Latin prose, as it evolved from its classical base from six hundred CE into the thirteenth century, as intelligible and interesting at each stage of its development as the literature of our own time. By its grasp of the relations between vulgar Latin's evolution and its contemporary audience, *Literatursprache und Publikum*, when it appeared, gave a more vivid picture of social realities than a sociologist could have done.

This, of course, was one of Auerbach's great strengths. He does not leave the present behind. The study of history comprises not just what lies in the past but what remains actual ("mit Einschluss des jeweils Gegenwärtigen").[4] "Wirklichkeit" is a favorite word, better translated as "actuality" or "worldly actualization" than as "reality." Writers of any period are pervaded by contemporary secular pressures and expectations: their "irdisch" character is made clear by Auerbach, even and especially when his topics are the Christian-inspired *sermo humilis*, or Dante's fusion of the "low" vernacular with the sublime themes of his epic, or the religious layer of the *passio* concept.

Literary mimesis, then, is more than a pale Platonic copy of realities.[5] And since every major literary work is defined by the fact that its style infers personality and the impact of social forces on it—or, more precisely, infers what turns character into destiny, into a player with a conspicuous role on the stage of the world—Auerbach is able to apply the same analytic instruments to medieval authors as to Virginia Woolf and Modernist literature. His knowledge of and respect for historical difference, on the one hand, and his—never mechanical—application of clear and probative concepts with an inbuilt connection between literature and society revived the hope that an authentic rather than antiquarian or tendentious literary history might be possible.

Auerbach achieved this with very little discussion of theory: he takes what he needs primarily from Vico, who held that we can understand only what we have made, and history ("civil society," "the world of nations") is what we have made. The proper study of mankind is mankind, but inclusive of its imaginative fertility, its gods and other worlds. Add to this creativeness language itself in its Babel-like variety, and particularly the fact that European culture was largely dependent on the change of classical Latin from "father tongue" and elite scholarly medium into a "mother tongue" or "lingua del pane." This living Latin is gradually diversified and further transformed under the impact of the national spirit, as the Romance languages become sophisticated literary vernaculars.

The apparatus of speculative instruments Auerbach deploys is, then, surprisingly small. If we look away from his subdued Hegelian perspective concerning humanity's self-realization through an odyssey called history—subdued by Auerbach in that, while he accepts a progressive dynamic, he thinks the periodization encouraged by *Geistesgeschichte* is too abstract—we find that he works primarily with two large concepts taken from social and religious history respectively. One is the *genera dicendi* doctrine of levels of style, based on the proper (hierarchic) correspondence of subject matter and diction. The other is the uneasy tension of that doctrine with the meta-allegorical character of Christian figural typology, which allows the most humble reality to enter literature and produce a decisive mixture of styles (*Stilmischung*). What makes both concepts moving and persuasive beyond the remarkable learning backing them up is that the first implies a sense of decorum or "aesthetic dignity" one always felt in Auerbach as a person, while the second implicates, as a wonderful essay on "Philologie der Weltliteratur" makes clear, his own historical situation.

Auerbach had an affinity with religious minds in the medieval era that developed a powerfully synthesizing rather than rejectionist view of secular history. History, although deemed the temporal space of exile, displayed a providential concreteness. For Christians, the figures and stories of the "Old" Testament were fulfilled, not abrogated, by the New Dispensation and augured a final if delayed historical fulfillment; for Auerbach, the plenitude came from the nearly inexhaustible variety of humanity and its creations. At the same time, Auerbach's personal diaspora, counterpointing that fullness, resonates to an ascetic notion of universality that views the scholar's *patria* as the earth, rather than the nation—if home is anywhere. What is gained here is a motivation for contemporary scholarship, a view of the past less distancing and more redemptive (in Walter Benjamin's sense) than was propagated by European cosmopolitanism in the aftermath of the Enlightenment.

One cannot escape the irony that it is a Jewish scholar who embodies this unusual combination of characteristics explicitly inspired in the first place by his reading of the Christian Fathers, their post-Pauline, anti-Marcionic saving of the text of the Septuagint. It must remain an open question whether Auerbach could have drawn a similar perspective from his own tradition's exegetical literature had he known it better. In the Jewish tradition, Midrash, the exegetical and imaginative filling-in of the Bible's elliptical narratives, is put in the service of an inventive law-finding and ethical exemplification governing the entirety of daily life. The ideal of a just and sacred polity was maintained into its minutest regulations despite the destruction of the Temples; Jewish hope was deeply shaped both by the condition of exile and by the belief in a messianic ingathering that would negate the diaspora. There would be an end-state, an ingathering not of the Jews alone but of all nations unified by a God whose Name is One.

Auerbach's analysis in *Mimesis* of the Binding of Isaac (the "Akedah") is a brief if immensely suggestive speculation on how a religious community is formed. The means by which that community binds itself are the unity and consecration of a literary source with measureless interpretability. Although there is no generalized theory of hermeneutics in Auerbach, that even the most secular politics needs a textual grounding is shown by a technique of "exegetical bonding."[6] But this is also where dogmatic law enters to limit and institutionalize. The political theology of nationalism tends to take over and mandate a single, exclusive narrative and interpretation. Auerbach does not dwell on this turn of events, for his historical knowledge tells him that, over time, the complex, flexible, indeed uncontainable daemon of linguistic process always materially subverts a strict sociopolitical uniformity.

As I write this, a memory comes back. Esther, the newly installed queen of King Ahasuerus, who unbeknownst to him is a Hebrew, is persuaded by her uncle Mordecai to bring Haman's plot to kill the Jews to the king's attention. In chapter 4 of the Book of Esther she decides: "I will go to the king, though it is against the law; and if I perish, I perish." She gives orders for a complex of ritual preparations, and the next chapter portrays her standing in the line of the king's sight, within the "inner court of the king's palace . . . and when the king saw Queen Esther standing in the court, she found favor in his sight and he held out to Esther the golden scepter that was in his hand. Then Esther approached and touched the top of the scepter."

We were studying, I believe, Racine's dramatization of the biblical story, and I must have taken Esther's comment on the danger of approaching the king too lightly. For Auerbach emphasized it could have been fatal for her to appear before the king, even to this extent, without having being summoned. He made me realize that everything in the unfolding of this episode implies danger and recalls the more primal risk of coming too near to God. I took the lesson, but today I associate his perceptiveness with his sense of decorum previously mentioned, and which is also conspicuous, for example, in his exposition of French neoclassicism's extreme separation of levels of style.

In this, as *Mimesis* demonstrates, Shakespeare differed fundamentally from Racine and Corneille.[7] Their tragedies were always performed as if the king were present. Auerbach, moreover, was intent on valuing not only the present as a historical category, but also Presence itself— how, through literature or ritual, it shapes human behavior. In "Philology of World Literature," he describes his era as a *kairos* moment: thus he is also present to himself as an interpreter, aware of his own situation vis-à-vis the knowledge explosion after more than a century of historicism, aware too of the enigmatic richness of daily life that challenges the formalism of the *genera dicendi*. Auerbach's concern that forms and distinctions, whether positive or negative, might fade away, makes it especially exciting to follow the motion of his ductile mind as he reflects on the exact, sinuous weave of Woolf's imagination threading its way from one person's interior to another, trying like *To the Lighthouse*'s Mrs. Ramsey to hold everything together.

Auerbach did not reveal much about his own past except for a few anecdotes concerning his exile in Turkey. I do not recall them in detail, but they betrayed a subsurface rivalry with Leo Spitzer, his precursor there, who had migrated with relative ease to a professorship at Johns Hopkins.[8] Auerbach had eventually to follow a more difficult career path in America: he taught first at Pennsylvania State University, was then invited to the Princeton Institute for Advanced Studies on a temporary basis, and through the efforts of Henri Peyre recruited for the French department at Yale. About his life in Germany, what has stayed with me is only the experience of his family during the great inflation. His father (or a friend) had financed an umbrella factory; eventually that money must have been totally lost, for he was offered as a final payment one of the umbrellas.

In retrospect, I find it remarkable that the issue of Jewishness did not come up. But Auerbach was clearly from a fully assimilated home, and I gathered that his radical cosmopolitan point of view did not incline him to any form of Zionism, despite the personal exile. Concerning that quiet, secular radicalism, Henri Peyre recalls Auerbach's "grand faible" for Montaigne and quotes his remarkable sentence on that writer: "N'est-ce pas être grand que d'avoir été le premier, peut-être le seul, à nous avoir enseigné comment vivre sur terre, sans autres conditions que celle de la vie?"[9]

Because of Auerbach's sabbatical, our conversations were interrupted. He died prematurely before we could resume our friendship. Surely, even had I not come to know him personally he would have exerted a strong influence on my work. Auerbach's combination of *esprit de finesse* and immense learning has remained for me the abiding and most influential testimony of humanistic scholarship.

What are the ingredients that contribute to Auerbach's appeal for many who generally find scholars of such breadth of knowledge and range of reference too daunting? There is, as I have hinted, an aesthetic factor, always hard to define: in other respects, both Spitzer and Curtius were his equals. They possessed his erudition, were also

177

interested in personality, and lived very much, perhaps even too much for their liking, in the present. Spitzer, with possibly a greater philological knowledge, and underrated as scholarly model, is always looking for psychological and linguistic clues to provide a key to personality; he aspires to solve a literary or linguistic riddle and often overwhelms the reader with an overflow of examples. Curtius also displays encyclopedic learning but differs from Spitzer by organizing it as a treasure comprised of "topoi" that are both analytic instruments and indispensable literary building blocks incorporated and transmitted by exceptional writers like Dante and Goethe. Given the political events of the 1930s, the contemporary actualization of that treasure was in jeopardy. *Memoria* had to flee, like Astrea, not into the heavens but into the refuge of scholarship. After the war, Curtius wrote many fine essays accommodated to a broadly educated public, and he could have had a formative rather than informative influence in America.

There is something special, however, about Auerbach's relation to prose. His own, of course, but also what he deals with so expertly, the prose of the Middle Ages, the French seventeenth century, the modern realistic novel. He certainly learned from Eduard Norden, yet Norden did his best work within the specialty of *Kunstprosa* and *Altertumswissenschaft*. I can only suggest that Auerbach, while not necessarily more great-hearted or empathic than these other scholars, enjoyed the itinerary, as it were, the spaciousness and variety prose allowed: he foresaw a prosaic modern era but did not regret it as such, only a tendency toward standardization. This makes his tone border on the elegiac in "Philology of World Literature," which is an envoi to as well as a celebration of the expansive, perspectival historical scholarship Goethe already recognized with the concept of "Weltliteratur."

Where are we, then, fifty and more years after Auerbach's passing? What remains is not only his eloquent understanding of the historical density of literary texts together with the social function of interpretation, but the chastened way in which he controlled his own forebodings. Forced into nomadism, he was surprisingly affirmative; at the same time, he sidestepped the utopian aspect of Hegel's revision of Vico, which envisaged history's progress toward a final actualization of humanity's self-expressive potential. Auerbach did go so far as to call historicism's enrichment of the human adventure, its revelation of diversity, an inspiring scholarly myth: only a myth, that is, but one valid for his time.

From the position of exile he asks, in effect, for a *carpe kairos*. How different this is from the elegiac strain in recent conceptions of history-writing: consider Michel de Certeau's assertion that the working of history is a "work of death and against death." Auerbach's contemplative literary humanism exerts its own, more than positivistic pressure on the contemporary. Through him historicism seeks to generate by purely scholarly means testimony to oppose the forces of uniformity and intolerance.

I wonder, in that respect, how well he knew Walter Benjamin's philosophy of history, with its Marxist-inspired yet mystical theory of hope. It posits a weak messianic power locked in the past, in the realm of the repressed, anonymous, forgotten. The hope prevails for a restitution, an imaginative act that will liberate a spark, however weak, of that power and bring a retroactive measure of justice. Yet Auerbach, while recognizing the anagogic impulse in humanism as in religion, maintains a penultimate view, patiently appraising each literary-historical phase as it passes, spreading its exemplary texts before us like an inexhaustible feast. I rarely feel in his work a compulsion to prove: to teach, yes, but the *delectare* always accompanies the *docere*.

NOTES

1. A short version of this autobiographical essay was originally written for Yale's Koerner Center for Emeriti Faculty and a program on "Intellectual Trajectories" initiated by David Apter.

2. Of close friends at that time, I should mention Marcel Mendelson, also a refugee, whom I had met at Queens College, CUNY, and who, like myself, went on to graduate studies at Yale. A talented linguist, uneasy with his cosmopolitanism, he eventually settled in Israel where he became a teacher of French literature but also initiated courses in the history of art at Bar Ilan. We often studied together and have continued to do so. Joel Orent, whom I encountered during my army years, where we read the book of Job together, graduated from the Jewish Theological Seminary, spent a short time as a rabbi, tried to reconcile Western and Eastern forms of religion, became a fine portrait photographer, and very "frumm." At that time I also met Arthur Cohen and envied his commitment to have German Jewish thought inspire (perhaps even create) a modern Jewish theology. I often read Abraham Heschel during those years and spent an afternoon with him talking about poetry.

3. Between *The Unmediated Vision* and *Wordsworth's Poetry* I did not give up writing verse and also went against the contemporary tide by reviews that questioned the turn to confessionalism and an aggressively intimate diction. The new, supervernacular orthodoxy was leading to bouts of exhibitionistic self-exposure as well as to a forgetfulness of the high Romantic style.

4. I take this opportunity to name Nehama Leibowitz (see also p. 149), whose seminar I audited while teaching at the Hebrew University in 1959; Judah Goldin, after he came to

Yale; and private sessions with Bible scholars Michael Fishbane, Moshe Greenberg, Uri Simon, during visits to Israel; and Daniel Boyarin when he spent a semester at Yale. David Stern's understanding of the contribution Midrash might make to secular criticism, and the matchless erudition yet open quality of thought in David Weiss Halivni's books, were important to me at a later stage, as were Moshe Idel's writings on the Kabbala.

5. Dr. Phil. D. Hartmann, *Das Buch Ruth in der Midrash-Literatur: Ein Beitrag zur Geschichte der Bibelexegese* (Leipzig: Bär & Hermann, 1901).

6. Its vast literary circumspection went much further than I could, yet Auerbach omitted most Romantic and post-Romantic poetry. Like E. R. Curtius, he lessened the gulf between medieval and modern, making in that way a distinctive contribution to Modernism—also by a mimesis concept based on the post-Christian realism of the nineteenth- and twentieth-century novel.

7. There exist possibilities, however limited their public impact may be, of an intervention by literary scholars using their knowledge to combat disastrous ideological falsifications. E. R. Curtius's *European Literature and the Latin Middle Ages*, written during the Nazi years, though published afterward, was an attempt to counter the National Socialist purge of Latinity as a component of German culture. A more direct, earlier example of scholarly engagement is Leo Spitzer's 1918 tract *Anti-Chamberlain* (on H. Stewart Chamberlain's racist essays). Spitzer remarks that his response is (I translate) "the purely scholarly protest of an academic specialist" and is needed as an antidote to "the toxins of race hatred" ("Völkerverhetzung").

8. René Wellek, already writing his magisterial *History of Modern Criticism*, and as chair of Yale's graduate program in comparative literature, did not tire of emphasizing this debt.

9. Coleridge claimed that his unfinished poem on Xanadu was based on a dream interrupted by a "letter from Porlock."

10. This was not my first attempt at having an essay published. I submitted, unsuccessfully, a consideration of Herman

Wouk's *Marjorie Morningstar* to *Commentary*, making a strong case for it, though comparing it not very favorably with Henry Roth's *Call It Sleep*. So I did have some Americanist tendencies in me!

11. The title essay of the book was a talk first given at a small symposium at Yale in late 1965, before the famous structuralism conference of 1966 at Johns Hopkins where Derrida made his American debut. Jacques Ehrmann organized the Yale meeting, assisted by Morris Dickstein and Richard Klein. Among others present, though not all presenting, were Paul de Man, J. Hillis Miller, Eugenio Donato, and Ralph Cohen.

12. *The Hooligan's Return: A Memoir* (New York: Farrar, Straus, and Giroux, 2003), 175. The next excerpt is from p. 291.

13. I should quote, however, a canny observation of Ortega y Gasset. He writes in *Toward a Philosophy of History* (New York: Norton, 1941), 35–36: "Everything ancient that is no longer understood seems to acquire an electric charge of mysticism that transforms it into a religious phenomenon."

14. Geoffrey Hartman, "War in Heaven," in *The Fate of Reading and Other Essays* (New Haven, Conn.: Yale University Press, 1976).

15. On a more problematic level, tradition comprised racial identity. At best, as in Hyppolite Taine, this was still understood as raciness: as cultural characteristics formed, sustained, and confirmed over an immemorial stretch of time, rather than transmitted by a mysterious and superior bloodline.

16. It could even have a near-blasphemous side. Primo Levi in *The Periodic Table* tells an anecdote about his laboratory in March 1939. His fellow workers were trying to extract and identify certain elements. "Through the murk and in the busy silence, we heard a Piedmontese voice say: '*Nuntio vobis gaudium magnum. Habemus ferrum.*' 'I announce to you a great joy. We have iron.'. . . [A] few days earlier an almost identical solemn announcement . . . had raised to Peter's Throne Cardinal Eugenio Pacelli."

17. While Frye recognizes the ubiquity of popular literature, and especially the trickle-down tendency of "snobbish" romance patterns, he gives a devastating critique of what he names "social adjustment" mythologies. See in *The Secular Scripture: A Study of the Structure of Romance* (Cambridge, Mass.: Harvard University Press, 1976), the chapter on "The Recovery of Myth," 166–70.

18. Two large schemes competed to digest the fact that the onset of literature, with Homer and Greek tragedy on the one side and the Hebrew Bible on the other, seemed so much stronger than what followed (with a few exceptions, preeminently Shakespeare). One scheme was called (by Frye) the "Great Western Butterslide," because it held that genius had declined in imaginative, while improving in intellectual, power as civilization, sunlike, moved from East to West. The other, also struggling with a sense of art's decadence, especially after Enlightenment concerns about the corrupting, antiscientific influence of imagination, pictured a compensatory, geopolitical Progress of the Spirit of Liberty from Greek beginnings to the freedom-loving British and Northern (and, in the Germany-to-be, resistantly Allemanic) parts of the globe. British colonialism as the evangel that set men free! A third scheme, however, associated chiefly with the Romantic period, emphasized originality ("original composition") by claiming, in effect, that the North (West) had its own genius loci, or that, as one writer put it hyperbolically, "Who knows whether the sun one day will not rise in the north?"

19. I first heard of Benjamin through Peter Szondi, when invited to give my "Structuralism" lecture at his recently founded Comparative and General Literature Seminar at the Free University of Berlin in the fall of 1966, and remember visiting with him his favorite "Bücherstube" to acquire what of Benjamin was available at that time, in particular the writings edited by Theodor Adorno. That occasion was my first visit to a German university.

20. In 1960, I published a little book on Malraux in a series on modern European writers edited by Erich Heller. In addition to a consideration of Malraux's theory of art, it attempted a close, sequential reading, thematic and stylistic, of his novels.

21. This from one of our most passionate and eloquent critics, close in background and age to myself, who chooses to view it all as stemming from "a characteristic Jewish rebellion against the paternalistic, logocentric burden of textuality of Mosaic-Talmudic prescription." George Steiner, *Errata: An Examined Life* (New Haven, Conn.: Yale University Press, 1998), 148. There is an ironic symmetry here between Steiner and myself, if one considers my argument (see p. 74) that, to the contrary, Derrida's deconstruction is a mode of "saving the [canonical] text," one basic to Judaism.

22. See, e.g., the articles by Shmuel Trigano in *Controverses* 1 (Paris: Editions de l'Éclat, 2006), critical of those he calls *alter-mondialistes*.

23. On this, consult George Steiner, *After Babel: Aspects of Language and Translation* (Oxford: Oxford University Press, 1975).

24. See the "Entretien" in *Le Monde* of August 19, 2004. Parts of my discussion here of Derrida have been published as "Homage to *Glas*" in *Critical Inquiry* 33 (Winter 2007): 344–61.

25. An important scene from Genet's *Journal of a Thief* that depicts a border crossing makes its way into later pages of *Glas* but is already anticipated on the first page by the "aigle . . . blanc" ("white eagle") mention. Cf. Geoffrey Hartman, *Criticism in the Wilderness*, 2nd ed. (New Haven, Conn.: Yale University Press, 2007), 208–11.

26. The difference, however, between a linguistic and a philological perspective is noted by Peter Szondi when he complains about "an Esoterics à la Derrida . . . (which I hate to mention, because I like Derrida very much), when one plays fantastic variations on texts in the manner of Liszt on themes of Bach.

Meanwhile, philology is made to stand in the corner." Letter to Herbert Dieckmann of November 20, 1970. My translation.

27. See Mikhail Bakhtin, *The Dialogic Imagination: Four Essays* (on the theory of the novel and the philosophy of language), a scholarly edition prepared and, with Caryl Emerson, translated by Michael Holquist from M. M. Bakhtin's *Voprosy estetiki I literatury* (Austin: University of Texas Press, 1981). Holquist's work, translating and advocating Bakhtin, became even more important to Yale's intellectual ferment when, with Katerina Clark, he returned to the university in 1986.

28. Robert Desnos, "Rrose Sélavy," in *L'Aumonyme* (1923). By adding and spelling out an (extra) *r* in "Rose," the pseudo-homonym *Eros* is created. Derrida is also at times intensely intrigured—like Artaud, whose work he often interpreted—with the mystical as well as pictorial impact of alphabetic letters. It may have a relevance to *Glas* that Artaud described the *H* as two columns . . . two lateral sides of Being, each of which ascends uniquely."

29. The most recent example, perhaps tongue-in-cheek, is Alain Badiou's "La puissance de l'ouvert: discours sur la nécessité de la fusion de l'Allemagne et de la France." In *Circonstances* 2 (Paris: Editions Lignes, 2004).

30. For Derrida's last and most moving statement on this, see the already mentioned "Entretien" in *Le Monde*. Derrida had previously joined Jürgen Habermas in what was at once a protest against President Bush's policy on the eve of the Iraq war and a *credo*-like declaration praising the secularism of Europe.

31. *"ce qui est resté d'un Rembrandt déchiré en petits carrés bien réguliers, et foutus aux chiottes"*

32. The two columns dividing Derrida's page (a citation, too, "stolen" from Genet's essay *"Ce qui est resté d'un Rembrandt . . ."*) are as antimonumental, say, as Oldenburg's fantastic architectural sketches. The two columns never balance out; the impression made resembles more the Talmud's accreted

page than a Greek temple's stately architecture. There is, as the preceding pages have shown, a radical obliquity of content and phrasing, a border crossing of themes and words. In semiotic terms, the difference between marked and unmarked (*reste* and *resté*), or voiced and unvoiced, also indicates an unresolved equation or unstable equilibrium, a meaning-producing principle of differentiation.

33. In strange contrast to that thesis, de Man mentions Kafka as a major modern writer, along with Hemingway, Lawrence, and Gide, none of whom were Nazi favorites. For my full analysis, see "Judging Paul de Man" in *Minor Prophecies: The Literary Essay in the Culture Wars* (Cambridge, Mass.: Harvard University Press, 1991), 123–48.

34. In "egotisée" I hear also "egodicée" (egodicy, after the analogy of theodicy), which is, I believe, a coinage Derrida uses.

35. See, for my quotes, Paul de Man's *Blindness and Insight* (1971). My last quote is from the essay on "Literary History and Literary Modernity." The above paragraphs are revised from what I wrote in the prefatory pages to *A Critic's Journey* (1999), where I add that in *The Unmediated Vision* "I accepted modernity as a period term and did not recognize its link to a pattern that repeated itself in literary history."

36. It was indeed unusual to find, in the States, a philosophic mind of this caliber honoring literature. De Man's version of deconstruction claimed, in effect, that literature was more philosophical than philosophy. Both disciplines practiced a labor of the negative; literature, however, "knew" it could not reach an unmediated truth, whatever the author's desires or pretensions. Criticism too, by introducing linguistic terms into its language of description, avoided ideological mystification by showing that every truth is not only phenomenal but referred: it cannot leave words behind but remains mediated as well as mediating. Yet deconstruction, seeking to demonstrate that authors are often blind to the way their text questions itself, and that this tension between blindness and insight affected philosophical

even more than literary works, produces a tight and difficult discourse as conceptually demanding as a negative theology, though remaining entirely secular.

37. The literary, in de Man's own attack on aesthetic ideology, was precisely that which resisted the "aesthetic" (or took the latter's name), including such political delusions, for example, as the fascist concept of the organic national state.

38. On the concept of experience, see Martin Jay, *Songs of Experience: Modern American and European Versions of a Universal Theme* (Los Angeles: University of California Press, 2005).

39. W. K. Wimsatt, *Day of the Leopards: Essays in Defense of Poems* (New Haven, Conn.: Yale University Press, 1976). Hillis Miller's essay had first been presented at the 1965 Yale symposium previously mentioned.

40. Owen Fiss, "Objectivity and Interpretation," *Stanford Law Review* 34 (1982): 763. For Fiss, the main antagonist, however, was Stanley Fish. Yet the Yale Law School continued to welcome literary scholars: Peter Brooks, somewhat later, team-taught courses there and went on to demonstrate the mutual relevance of legal and literary issues. At Cardozo Law School, Richard Weisberg, a legal as well as literary scholar, also troubled by "postmodernist" indeterminacies, encouraged a "poethics" and initiated a Law and Literature movement. Thomas Greene, premier Renaissance scholar and one of my closest friends at Yale, who called himself a child of the New Criticism with a tincture of Auerbachian historicism, also had his reservations. He once objected to an ambiguating interpretation of mine in the following terms: "I find [Hopkins's] 'The Shepherd's Brow' less taxing and unresolved than you do, in fact not unresolved at all. Sometimes, I think, one has to resist the temptation of the double reading of a word, which can in certain contexts become a trap. Coherence is really the determining factor, at least for me, and if the poem falls into place without the addition of a double interpretation, then one has to discipline one's hermeneutic inventiveness."

41. Frank Rich, op-ed in the "Week in Review" section of the *New York Times*, Sunday, June 19, 2005.

42. I should add that at the end of my second year of graduate studies, and before taking up a Fulbright, I spent six weeks of the summer at the Indiana School of Letters, previously the Kenyon School, founded by one who can be truly called a man of letters, John Crowe Ransom. I was too ignorant at that time to recognize the stellar cast the school offered: Allen Tate, Delmore Schwartz, Francis Ferguson, and Austin Warren (the latter replaced after two weeks by Robert Fitzgerald, poet and distinguished translator of Homer and Virgil). I studied only with Ferguson, an eye-opening teacher of Shakespeare; with Warren, on religion and literature; and with Fitzgerald. Tate I gave up after he showed no interest in my fledgling attempts at poetry. I still remember the heady atmosphere, and its memory had something to do with wishing to be associated with Murray Krieger's enterprise.

43. There were many other signs of renewal. I restrict myself to the older generation and mention only, as symptomatic, and to please myself, John Irwin's transformation of the *Georgia Review*; Ralph Cohen's founding of *New Literary History*; other new journals like *Diacritics*, *Critical Inquiry*, and *Representations*; Stanley Cavell crossing over, as philosophical thinker, into film and literature; Richard Rorty's and Richard Bernstein's engagement with Continental modes of philosophizing; Clifford Geertz's understanding of the relation between structures of art and social institutions; Hayden White's views about the mediated (narrative and tropic) aspect of history writing; and the first translations of Maurice Blanchot's work into English. Significant discussions of Bataille, Blanchot, and Foucault appeared, and both gender and media studies took off, with many women scholars in the lead. For Europe, I restrict myself to adding (1) Hans-Georg Gadamer's and Paul Ricoeur's revival and extension of a hermeneutics embracing the entirety of the humanistic disciplines; (2) Peter Szondi's scholarly yet

engaged criticism that updated all the conventional branches of literary study, poetics, hermeneutics, as well as illuminating literature's biographical context (see his exegetical work on Paul Celan); (3) Tzvetan Todorov, Gerard Genette, and Jean Starobinski, for groundbreaking books versed in the history of rhetoric and poetics; (4) Umberto Eco's descriptive theory of the structured openness of the work of art; (5) Julia Kristeva's concept of intertextuality, developing a central insight of Mikhail Bakhtin; and (6) Aleida and Jan Assmann's historical and analytic grounding of the concept of cultural memory. Later, Sigrid Weigel, Karl-Heinz Barck, and the Berlin "Zentrum für Literaturforschung" also contributed actively to this.

44. This was an exaggeration, but only in the sense that the ancient cultures of the Middle East, among which Judaism arose, were represented by professorships like that of William Hallo, and that the Hebrew Bible was also, of course, the object of study in the divinity school and by teachers recruited from there to form the religious studies department in the 1960s.

45. While this memoir was being prepared for publication, I came across the notebook record of a dream that betrays, however self-deprecatingly, an identity wish. It signaled my desire to be a scholar who could assimilate or embody—be the child of—both Jewish and non-Jewish learning. The dream took place in Paris during the time Yale was to approve calling me back. I dreamt I was translating an ancient text, with Bill Wimsatt correcting me and my acknowledging at one point, "Yes, I know, I shall never quite lose my accent." But Margaret (Mrs. Wimsatt) turns to him and says: "Make me a *schlemiel* like that."

46. Mark Krupnick, *Jewish Writing and the Deep Places of the Imagination*, ed. Jean Carney and Mark Shechner (Madison: University of Wisconsin Press, 2005), 71.

47. *Criticism in the Wilderness*, 218.

48. For this "disarmed speech," see *Robert Antelme: Textes inédits / Sur L'espèce humaine / Essais et témoignages* (Paris:

Gallimard, 1996), 68. Cf. Blanchot in *The Writing of the Disaster*, trans. Ann Smock (Lincoln: University of Nebraska Press, 1986), 11: "May words cease to be arms, means of action, means of salvation." Sarah Kofman picks up on these admonitions to speak from the position of powerlessness in *Paroles suffoquées*.

49. Rob Walker, "Cross Selling," *New York Times Magazine*, March 6, 2005.

50. For the theory, see "Structuralism: The Anglo-American Adventure," in *Beyond Formalism* (New Haven, Conn.: Yale University Press, 1970), 18–20.

51. The occasional cause of one of my most interesting lecture trips outside of Europe was related to political events. In 1985, Hillis Miller and I received invitations from Uruguay. The military regime had been sidelined, and it occurred to a cosmopolitan scholar of literature and semiotics in Montevideo, Lisa Block de Behar, to mark the new sense of liberated speech by (believe it or not) inviting a set of notorious deconstructionists. Lisa never said as much, but that is my suspicion. There was only one snag. The University of Montevideo, or whoever was needed to support the invitation, was not enthusiastic. For after the demise of the regime, the trend was to the left, and the United States was not in the best repute. Lisa prevailed by finding other sponsors, including the National Public Library in Montevideo. It was there, in an opulent chamber, that I gave what was basically a Jewish studies talk, "The Struggle with the Text," a modern midrashic exploration of Jacob's nighttime encounter with a mysterious mugger, from which encounter Jacob emerged as "Israel." On this visit to South America I also talked at Mendoza University in Argentina, where I was struck by the relationship of students and faculty, their sense of mutuality, a result of having suffered together a severe period of political oppression.

52. "Sonderheft," *Deutsche Vierteljahrsschrift für Literaturwissenschaft und Geistesgeschichte* (Stuttgart and Weimar, 1994).

53. While I have mentioned that in the 1970s the dominant emphasis in literary studies continued to be the concept of secularization (viewing literary progress or continuity in terms of a wholesale transfer from the religious to the nonreligious domain, fruitfully exemplified by M. H. Abrams's *Natural Supernaturalism* of 1971), there were signs, even within the surge of a New Historicism, of a less urbane, more anagogic approach to religious modes of interpretation. At Yale, two younger scholars, Leslie Brisman and Thomas Weiskel, began to be active. Brisman came from a strongly midrashic background, Weiskel from Protestant thought as it insisted that "the sublime still speaks to us" and engaged both Freud and Lacan. Weiskel died in a tragic accident toward the beginning of his career, leaving as his legacy one remarkable unfinished book, *The Romantic Sublime: Studies in the Structure and Psychology of Transcendence* (1976).

54. On the subject of graduate students I must add that while it is good that the university, in becoming open to different talents, has democratized and diversified itself, the resulting complex system of economic support, as well as pressures to find employment for many more students, have shifted the focus of basic decisions about the conditions of life in graduate school from the individual departments to the central administration. Curricular decisions remain with the departments, but as the workplace becomes very much a space for living, the student, and then apprentice teacher, senses that it is not the professor with whom he or she works but the deans and committees established by them that govern. Consequently the term "fellowship" changes its meaning or loses it entirely. The student on fellowship should be considered a fellow, that is, an associate of the faculty, but that same student realizes quickly enough that the faculty has a very limited say in conditions that affect the workplace. No wonder students begin to feel like employees of the central administration rather than fellows in a fellowship comprising the faculty they work with and perhaps admire. It is

not surprising, then, that in times of labor unrest the idea of solidarity with a union is not only emotionally attractive but appears quite logical. (Max Weber, remarking on the "Americanization" of *Wisssenschaft* in Germany circa 1917, notes that it is becoming a capitalistic operation insofar as the "assistant" is dependent on management, and he uses the analogy of the employee in a factory.) The real union, one that would join faculty and graduate students on matters not exclusively economic, cannot come about unless the faculty itself is more involved in what used to be considered private or the sole responsibility of the student. Yet to take on that burden by a type of self-sponsored organization may not be feasible without some sacrifice of the faculty member's time previously dedicated to scholarship.

55. See, however, the title essay of *The Longest Shadow.*

56. One interesting and independent documentary extension arising from the work of the Fortunoff archive is that Nathan Beyrak, Yale's coordinator of Holocaust-witness taping in Israel, founded Words and Images in 1994 to actively conduct video interviews in depth with Jewish writers of international distinction. Helping this project as cochair and literary consultant brought me closer to Nathan, and also to Eleonora Lev, the Israeli novelist, in charge of the essential research for each interview. Words and Images so far has links to Ben-Gurion University and the National Library in Israel, as well as to the Institute for Jewish Studies at the University of Antwerp.

57. This, and the quotes that follow, come from *Mauro Ceolin: Interview by Ivan Quaroni—Story by Tiziano Scarpa* (Milan: Joan & Levi, 2006), 25–47.

NOTES TO APPENDIX

1. This essay was originally a talk for the *Zentrum für Literaturforschung* under the direction of Sigrid Weigel and Karl-Heinz Barck.

2. I was surprised to hear Auerbach remark that he had almost omitted the first chapter from the book, and that in deference to pleas by "the ladies" kept it in.

3. Henri Peyre published in 1977 an affectionate and detailed appreciation of his colleague. See "Erich Auerbach (1892–1957) Romanist" in *Lebensbilder aus Hessen Bd. 1: Marburger Gelehrte in der ersten Hälfte des 20. Jahrhunderts*, ed. Ingeborg Schnack (Marburg: Veröffentlichungen der Historische Kommission für Hessen, 1977), 10–21.

4. "Philologie der Weltliteratur," in *Gesammelte Aufsätze zur Romanischen Philologie* (Bern: Francke Verlag, 1967).

5. Auerbach told me (and I am sure others) of a sitter to whom a commissioned portrait is presented by the painter. The subject protests: "That doesn't look like me at all." To which the painter replies: "It's more like than you are" ("Es ist ähnlicher als Sie").

6. The phrase is used by David Apter, who demonstrates how crucial this was to Mao's own grand narrative while creating the new China. See Apter's *Revolutionary Discourse in Mao's Republic* (Cambridge, Mass.: Harvard University Press, 1994).

7. Shakespeare's model won out in England, but there were, as is well-known, countercurrents. For example, his contemporary Francis Bacon remarks, about a "high speech" of Seneca's ("too high for a heathen"), that "this would have done better in poesy, where transcendences are more allowed." See Bacon's essay "Of Adversity." Distinguishing prose from poetry in terms of subject matter is also a separate issue; Bacon's essays, though characterized by the mannered, aphoristic style of Seneca, are a step toward what became known as the "familiar" essay, a genre, as Bacon mentions on his dedication page, that comes home "to Men's Businesse, and Bosomes." Bacon nevertheless takes care to also publish his essays in Latin (which he calls "the Universall Language") in the hope they "may last, as long as Bookes last."

8. For Turkey as a "laboratory" shaping a conception of comparative literature that, through both Spitzer's and Auerbach's second migration, to the United States, was to influence that profession profoundly, see the informative article by Emily Apter, "Global *Translatio*: The 'Invention' of Comparative Literature, Istanbul, 1933," *Critical Inquiry* 29 (Winter 2003): 253–81. Apter does full justice to Spitzer's animating role.

9. Henri Peyre, "Erich Auerbach (1892–1957) Romanist," 16. "Is it not a great thing to have been the first, and perhaps the only one, to teach us how to live on earth without any other conditions except those of life itself?"